EYEWITNESS
WORLD WAR I

Signboard from Ypres station, 1916

British B.E.2c reconnaissance aircraft

Book that stopped a bullet

Early British "Hypo" gas helmet

German stereoscopic periscope

British "carcass" incendiary bomb

Pickelhaube (German military helmet)

German incendiary bomb, dropped during first air raid on London

Model of British motor ambulance used on the Western Front

Prussian
Iron Cross

EYEWITNESS

WORLD
WAR I

Written by
SIMON ADAMS

Photographed by
ANDY CRAWFORD

US Distinguished
Service Cross

British 0.303 in
Maxim Mark III
medium
machine gun

Wooden figurine
of Herbert Asquith,
British prime
minister from
1908 to 1916

Wooden figurine of
Grand Duke Nicholas,
commander in chief
of the Russian armies
at the start of the war

DK

British officer's compass

German steel helmet adapted for use with a telephone

Dummy rifles used by British Army recruits, 1914–15

REVISED EDITION

DK DELHI
Senior Editor Virien Chopra
Senior Art Editor Vikas Chauhan
Art Editor Tanvi Sahu
Assistant Editor Zarak Rais
Assistant Art Editor Prateek Maurya
Senior Picture Researcher Sumedha Chopra
Managing Editor Kingshuk Ghoshal
Managing Art Editor Govind Mittal
DTP Designers Pawan Kumar, Vikram Singh, Deepak Mittal
Jackets Designer Vidushi Chaudhry
Senior Jackets Coordinator Priyanka Sharma Saddi

DK LONDON
Senior Editor Michelle Crane
Senior Art Editor Sheila Collins
US Senior Editor Jennette ElNaggar
US Executive Editor Lori Cates Hand
Managing Editor Francesca Baines
Managing Art Editor Philip Letsu
Production Editor Jacqueline Street-Elkayam
Production Controller Jack Matts
Senior Jackets Designer Surabhi Wadhwa-Gandhi
Jacket Design Development Manager Sophia MTT
Publisher Andrew Macintyre
Associate Publishing Director Liz Wheeler
Art Director Karen Self
Publishing Director Jonathan Metcalf

Consultant Peter Doyle
Authenticity Reader Bianca Hezekiah

FIRST EDITION
Project Editor Patricia Moss
Art Editors Julia Harris, Rebecca Painter
Senior Editor Monica Byles
Senior Art Editors Jane Tetzlaff, Clare Shedden
Category Publisher Jayne Parsons
Managing Art Editor Jacquie Gulliver
Senior Production Controller Kate Oliver
Picture Research Sean Hunter
DTP Designers Justine Eaton, Matthew Ibbotson

This Eyewitness ® Guide has been conceived by Dorling Kindersley Limited and Editions Gallimard

This American edition, 2023
First American edition, 2001
Published in the United States by DK Publishing
1745 Broadway, 20th Floor, New York, NY 10019

Copyright © 2001, 2004, 2007, 2014, 2023 Dorling Kindersley Limited
DK, a Division of Penguin Random House LLC
23 24 25 26 27 10 9 8 7 6 5 4 3 2 1
001–336552–Dec/2023

A catalog record for this book is available from the Library of Congress.
ISBN 978-0-7440-8475-7 (Paperback)
ISBN 978-0-7440-8476-4 (ALB)

DK books are available at special discounts when purchased in bulk for sales promotions, premiums, fund-raising, or educational use. For details, contact: DK Publishing Special Markets, 1745 Broadway, 20th Floor, New York, NY 10019 SpecialSales@dk.com

Printed and bound in China

www.dk.com

French *Croix de Guerre* medal awarded for valor

British and German barbed wire

British steel helmet with visor

Mills bomb

German medical orderly's pouch

Contents

Artillery shells

Divided Europe

At the start of the 20th century, the countries of Europe were increasingly hostile to one another. While Britain, France, and Germany vied for trade and influence, Austria-Hungary and Russia both tried to dominate the Balkan states of southeast Europe. Military alliances, a naval arms race, and two Balkan wars in 1912–1913 made the political situation tense, but few predicted a war.

HMS *Dreadnought*

Britain's HMS *Dreadnought*, launched in 1906, outperformed every other battleship of the day. As a result, Germany, France, and other maritime nations began to build their own "Dreadnoughts," starting a worldwide naval armaments race.

Kaiser Wilhelm II

On becoming Kaiser (emperor) of Germany in 1888, Wilhelm II tried to turn Germany into a world power, but his aggressive policies and arrogant behavior upset other European nations, particularly Britain and France.

HMS Dreadnought *had a top speed of 21 knots.*

The German fleet

In 1898, Germany began an ambitious naval building program to challenge the supremacy of the British Royal Navy. Children played with tin battleships in their baths.

EUROPEAN RIVALRIES

In 1882, Germany, Austria-Hungary, and Italy signed the Triple Alliance to protect against invasion. Alarmed by this, France and Russia formed an alliance in 1894. Britain signed ententes (understandings) with France in 1904 and Russia in 1907. In 1915, Italy left the Triple Alliance and joined the Allied side. This map shows how the two rival groups divided Europe by 1915.

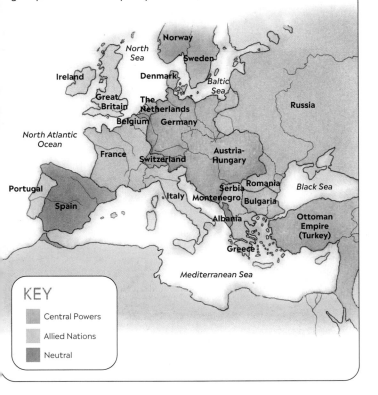

North Sea
Norway
Sweden
Ireland
Denmark
Baltic Sea
Great Britain
The Netherlands
North Atlantic Ocean
Belgium
Germany
Russia
France
Switzerland
Austria-Hungary
Portugal
Spain
Italy
Serbia
Montenegro
Romania
Bulgaria
Black Sea
Albania
Ottoman Empire (Turkey)
Greece
Mediterranean Sea

KEY

- Central Powers
- Allied Nations
- Neutral

Tsar Nicholas II of Russia (left), King George V of Britain (right)

Related royalty

George V of Britain, Wilhelm II of Germany, and Alexandra Feodorovna, wife of Tsar Nicholas II of Russia, were all cousins. They had the same grandmother, Queen Victoria of Britain.

> ## "This, the greatest of all wars, is not just another war, it is the last war!"
> —H. G. Wells, British author, The War That Will End War, October 1914

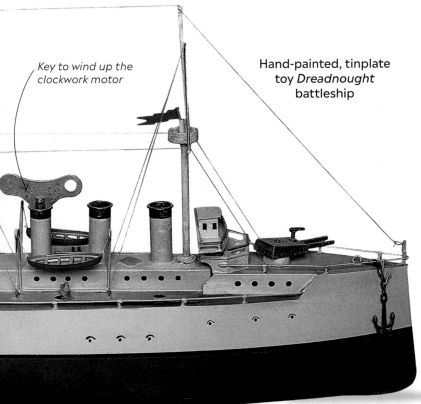

Key to wind up the clockwork motor

Hand-painted, tinplate toy *Dreadnought* battleship

The power house

This factory—in the Rhur valley of western Germany—belonged to the Krupp family, then the biggest arms supplier in the world. When Germany was unified in 1871, it was a largely agricultural nation. Within 30 years, Germany became the third largest industrial country in the world, after Britain and the US.

A fatal shot

On June 28, 1914, the heir to the Austro-Hungarian throne, Archduke Franz Ferdinand, was shot dead in Sarajevo, Bosnia. As Bosnia was claimed by neighboring Serbia, Austria-Hungary blamed Serbia for the assassination, and on July 28 declared war. Germany supported Austria-Hungary, Russia supported Serbia, and France supported Russia. When Germany invaded neutral Belgium on its way to France, Britain declared war on Germany. The Great War had begun.

The Austro-Hungarian Army

The Austro-Hungarian Empire had three armies—Austrian, Hungarian, and the "Common Army." There were 10 main languages that were spoken, leading to frequent communication difficulties.

Germany rejoices

Germany mobilized on August 1, declaring war against Russia that evening and against France on August 3. Many civilians (right) rushed to join the army in support of Kaiser and country.

Austro-Hungarian *Reiter* (Trooper) of the 8th Uhlan (Lancer) Regiment

The archduke and his wife Sophie sat in the back of the open-top car.

Princip fired at close range from the running board.

One day in Sarajevo

Believing that Bosnia should be part of Serbia, six assassins ambushed Archduke Ferdinand in Sarajevo. One threw a bomb at Ferdinand's car, but it bounced off and exploded minutes later. When Ferdinand and his wife visited the injured officers in the hospital, one of the assassins, Gavrilo Princip, mounted the royal car and shot the couple. The tragic event sparked the Great War.

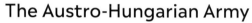

June 28 Archduke Franz Ferdinand is assassinated
July 5 Germany gives its ally Austria-Hungary total support

July 23 Austria-Hungary issues an ultimatum to Serbia that threatens Serbian independence

July 25 Serbia agrees to most of the demands
July 28 Austria-Hungary ignores Serbia's terms and declares war

July 30 Russia mobilizes in support of its ally Serbia
August 1 Germany mobilizes against Russia and declares war; France

German (above) and French (right) mobilization posters

Vive La France

The French Army mobilized on August 1. For many Frenchmen, the war was a chance to seek revenge for the German defeat of France in 1870–1871.

All aboard!

The German troops on this westbound train believed that the offensive against France would soon take them to Paris. French troops felt the same about Berlin.

mobilizes in support of ts ally Russia; Germany signs a treaty with Ottoman Turkey; Italy declares its neutrality

August 2 Germany invades Luxembourg

August 3 Germany declares war on France

August 4 Germany invades Belgium en route to France; Britain enters the war to safeguard Belgian neutrality

August 6 Austria-Hungary declares war on Russia

August 12 France and Britain declare war on Austria-Hungary

Christmas treat

The City of London Territorial Association sent each of its soldiers a canned plum pudding for Christmas in 1914.

War in the west

By 1905, fearing war on two fronts, Germany's Field Marshal Count Alfred von Schlieffen had developed a plan to knock France swiftly out of any war before turning against Russia. In August 1914, the plan went into operation. German troops crossed the Belgian border on August 4 and, by the end of the month, invaded northern France. At the Battle of the Marne on September 5, the German advance was held and pushed back. By Christmas 1914, the two sides faced stalemate on the Western Front, along a line from the Belgian coast in the north to the Swiss border in the south.

In the field

The British Expeditionary Force (BEF) had arrived in France by August 22, 1914. Its cavalry division included units of the Royal Horse Artillery, armed with the 13-pounder quick-firing Mark I gun. This particular gun (right) was used by E Battery Royal Horse Artillery in action at Binche, 10 miles (16 km) from Mons, Belgium, on the Western Front, where it fired the first British artillery round of the war.

Handle known as the handspike, which helps the gunners traverse (move) the gun in position

n retreat
Unable to block the German Army, Belgian soldiers with dog-drawn machine guns withdraw to Antwerp.

The Christmas truce
On December 24, 1914, soldiers in some areas on both sides of the Western Front lit candles and sang carols in their trenches. The next day, troops along the front observed a truce. Firing stopped, and soldiers from both sides crossed into no-man's-land to talk to their enemy and exchange cigarettes and other souvenirs. South of Ypres, Belgium, the two sides are known to have kicked a soccer ball about in no-man's-land. One year later, however, sentries on both sides were ordered to fire on anyone climbing out of enemy trenches.

British soldier shooting at enemy with a note saying "Christmas Eve—Got 'im!"

Eyewitness
Captain E. R. P. Berryman wrote a letter home describing the truce. This cartoon illustrates the absurdity of his situation—shooting the enemy one day and greeting them as friends the next.

German trench

Rope wrapped around recoil mechanism

British and German soldiers greeting each other on Christmas Day

The 13-pounder gun fired 12.5 lb (5.6 kg) shells a maximum distance of 17,700 ft (5,395 m).

The gun was made of metal and wood.

Heading for the front
By early September, German troops were only 25 miles (40 km) east of Paris. The city's military governor used 600 taxis to take 6,000 men to reinforce the front line.

Fighting men

The outbreak of war in August 1914 changed the lives of millions. Regular soldiers, older reservists, eager recruits, and unwilling conscripts were all caught up in the war. Some were experienced soldiers, but many had barely held a rifle before. Britain and France also heavily depended on armies recruited from their colonies.

France

Grand Duke Nicholas

In 1914, the Russian Army was led by the Tsar's uncle, Grand Duke Nicholas. As the Russian commander-in-chief, he dealt with the overall strategy of the war, and his generals directed the battles. The other warring countries had similar chains of command.

Wooden figurine of the Grand Duke Nicholas

Hat flaps could be pulled down to keep out the cold

Winter jerkin made of goatskin or sheepskin

British soldier 1914–1915

The British Army

At the start of war, the British Army contained just 247,432 regulars and 218,280 reservists. They wore a khaki uniform consisting of a single-breasted tunic, trousers, puttees or leggings worn to protect the shins, and ankle boots.

Short Magazine Lee Enfield (SMLE) Mark III rifle

Eastern allies

In Eastern Europe, Germany faced the vast Russian Army, as well as smaller armies from Serbia and Montenegro. In the Far East, German colonies in China and the Pacific Ocean were occupied by Japan, Australia, and New Zealand.

Russia

Colonial troops

Britain and France took recruits from their colonies in Africa, Asia, the Pacific, and the Caribbean. Many of these men had never left home before. The Annamites (Indo-Chinese) above, from French Indo-China, were stationed at Salonika, Greece, in 1916.

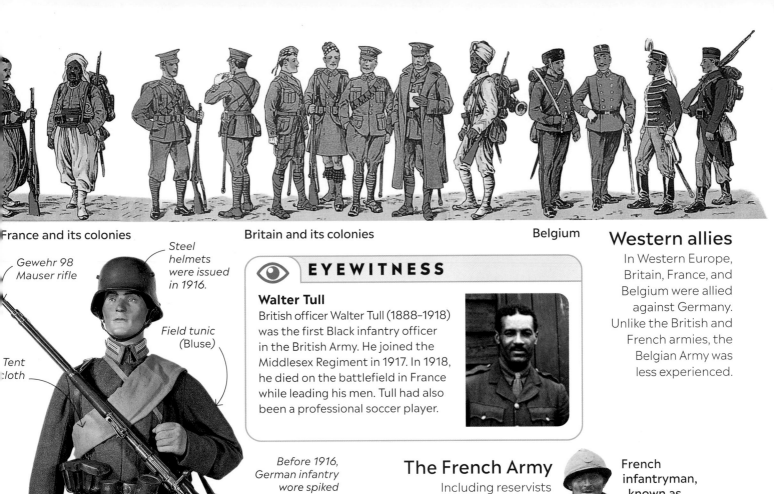

France and its colonies

Britain and its colonies

Belgium

Western allies

In Western Europe, Britain, France, and Belgium were allied against Germany. Unlike the British and French armies, the Belgian Army was less experienced.

Gewehr 98 Mauser rifle

Steel helmets were issued in 1916.

Field tunic (Bluse)

Tent cloth

👁 EYEWITNESS

Walter Tull
British officer Walter Tull (1888–1918) was the first Black infantry officer in the British Army. He joined the Middlesex Regiment in 1917. In 1918, he died on the battlefield in France while leading his men. Tull had also been a professional soccer player.

Before 1916, German infantry wore spiked helmets called Pickelhauben.

The French Army

Including reservists and colonial troops, the French Army totaled 3,680,000 trained men at the outbreak of war.

French infantryman, known as le poilu

Stick grenade

The German Army

In 1914, the German Army was the strongest in Europe, with 840,000 men. All men under the age of 45 were trained for military service and belonged to the reserve army. On calling up the reserves, the German Army could expand to more than four million trained men.

Gas mask

German soldier, 1916–1917

Lebel rifle

Serbia

Montenegro

Japan

Joining up

At the outbreak of war, unlike Europe's large armies of conscripts, Britain had only a small army made up of volunteers. On August 7, 1914, the Secretary of State for War, Lord Kitchener, asked for 100,000 new recruits in the press. The day after, huge lines formed at the recruiting offices.

War leader

Britain's prime minister in 1914, Herbert Asquith, was known as "the last of the Romans" because of his values of public duty and strong morals. This wooden figurine shows him dressed as an ancient Roman senator.

Small box respirator gas mask

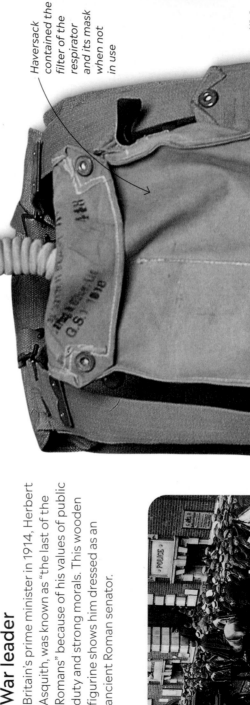

Haversack contained the filter of the respirator and its mask when not in use

Pouch contained three chargers (clips), each of

Line up here for "King and Country"

At the outbreak of war, men from the same area or industry joined Pals battalions so they could fight together. By mid-September, half a million men had volunteered.

The test

Every British recruit had a medical test to make sure he was fit to fight. Many failed the test, because of poor eyesight or ill health. Others were refused because they were under 19, although many lied about their age so that they could enlist.

"Your country needs you"

A portrait of Lord Kitchener was used as a recruiting and propaganda poster in 1914. Some 2,446,719 men had enlisted by 1916, but more were needed. The poster was also the inspiration for the renowned "Uncle Sam" poster in the US (see p.54).

Rations

Each soldier was given an emergency "iron ration," in case he was cut off from the daily supply of food. It included hard cookies, corned beef, tea, and stock cubes.

Cookies

Can for tea and stock cubes

Can of bully beef

Linen bag to store iron ration

Conscientious objectors

Certain religious groups objected to the war because they believed it was wrong to kill, and some socialists objected to fighting fellow workers. Both groups were known as conscientious objectors—those who refused to fight as it was against their beliefs. Some objectors served in noncombatant units, such as medical services. Sometimes, those who refused to enlist were handed white feathers as a mark of shame and a sign of cowardice.

Haversack used for soldier's gear when in the trenches

Entrenching tool handle

Razor case

Holdall

Boot laces

Bayonet

Knife

Cut-throat razor for shaving

Shaving brush

Fork

Spoon

Button stick

Water bottle

Soldier's small kit

The basic gear

British soldiers carried enough basic equipment to fight and to survive in the trenches: their rifle and bayonet, ammunition, a water bottle, and an entrenching tool to dig a shallow hole to take cover in. By 1917, they also carried a respirator in case of gas attacks. Their survival kit included cutlery, a washing kit, and spare clothes. Going into battle, they put the most needed items into a smaller haversack.

Troops from the colonies

European countries recruited many troops from their colonies in Asia and Africa. Over four million nonwhite troops served in the war, including one million Indian soldiers who fought with the British in Europe, Palestine, Mesopotamia, and Gallipoli, in regiments such as the 20th Deccan Horse (above). Colonies in Africa supplied 450,000 men to fight for France, including the *Tirailleurs Sénégalais* from Senegal and West Africa, while the Germans relied on African *Schutztruppe* soldiers to combat the Allies in Africa.

Stalemate

At the outbreak of war, both sides on the Western Front were equipped with powerful, rapid-firing artillery weapons and machine guns. These weapons made it dangerous for soldiers to fight in unprotected, open ground. So they dug defensive trenches and found themselves trapped in a static fight.

Front line of trenches

The front line

By December 1914, a network of trenches ran along the Western Front from the Belgian coast in the north down through eastern France to the Swiss border, 400 miles (645 km) in the south.

Entrenching tool cover

US M1910 entrenching tool

The first trenches

Early trenches were just deep furrows, providing minimal cover from enemy fire. Troops from the 2nd Scots Guards dug this trench near Ypres, Belgium, in October 1914.

Entrenching tools

Each soldier carried an entrenching tool. He used it to dig a scrape—a shallow trench—if he was caught out in the open by enemy fire. He could also use it to repair a trench damaged by an enemy artillery bombardment.

Positioning the trench

In the west, the Germans captured the high ground early in the war, allowing them to observe and fire on the French and British trenches positioned on the low ground. This made Allied attacks difficult. Here, troops from New Zealand are digging a trench during the Battle of the Somme in France in 1916.

Signposts

Each trench was signposted, often with its nickname, to avoid soldiers losing their way.

"Gradually the line became worse... We seemed to have been in one continuous nightmare of mud."
—*Captain F. C. Hitchcock, Leinster Regiment, British Army, November 2, 1915*

Home on the front line

The Germans constructed the most elaborate trenches, with superior facilities, and regarded them as the new German border. The trench base had wooden slats for keeping off the mud. These trenches were deeper, offering more protection, and some even had electric lights. The Allied trenches, by comparison, were generally poorly equipped.

TRENCH PLAN

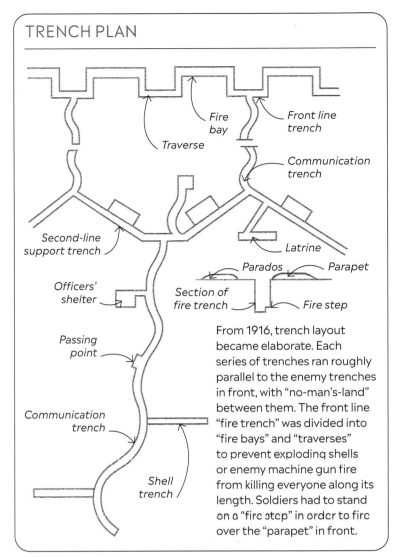

From 1916, trench layout became elaborate. Each series of trenches ran roughly parallel to the enemy trenches in front, with "no-man's-land" between them. The front line "fire trench" was divided into "fire bays" and "traverses" to prevent exploding shells or enemy machine gun fire from killing everyone along its length. Soldiers had to stand on a "fire step" in order to fire over the "parapet" in front.

Coping with the mud

In winter, rain, snow, and natural seepage soon filled trenches with water. Wooden slats, known as duckboards, were laid on the ground to keep soldiers' feet reasonably dry, but it was always muddy.

A little shelter

The trenches were usually very narrow and often exposed to the weather. These Canadian soldiers have built a makeshift canopy to shelter under.

Life in the trenches

Most of the work in the trenches was done at night. Patrols were sent out to observe and raid enemy trenches and to repair their own defenses. Dawn and dusk were the most likely times for an enemy attack, so all the troops stayed alert in the fire bays at these times. The days were usually quiet. Soldiers generally spent one week to 10 days in the front line then moved into the reserve lines, before finally going to the rear to rest. Here they bathed and were given clean clothes before returning to the trenches.

Officers' dugout

This recreation of an officers' dugout on the Somme, France, in fall 1916 shows the cramped conditions people endured in the trenches. The officer on the telephone is calling in artillery support for an imminent trench raid, while his weary comrade is asleep behind him on a camp bed.

Clean and tidy

Waterproofing boots and cleaning their gear (see p.15) was as much a part of life in the trenches as it was in the barracks back home. These Belgian soldiers cleaning their rifles knew that such tasks were essential to maintaining combat efficiency.

Trench cuisine

These French officers are dining well in a reserve trench. However, most soldiers ate canned food, bacon, bread, jam, and hard biscuits. Sometimes they cooked in the trenches or, on rare occasions, had hot meals brought up from behind the lines.

Funk holes

Ordinary soldiers—such as these British troops at Thiepval Wood on the Somme in 1916—spent their time off duty in "funk holes," carved out of the side of the trench, or under waterproof sheets.

Artists and poets

Some soldiers in the trenches wrote poems or made sketches. Many wrote long letters home, or kept a diary. These creative works are fascinating records of what trench life was really like. In 1916, the British government began to send official war artists, such as Paul Nash, to the front to record the war in paint.

The Menin Road (1918) by British war artist Paul Nash

Paints and brushes belonging to Paul Nash

Poem and self-portrait by the British poet and artist Isaac Rosenberg

Ready to fight

On the Western Front, soldiers in the front line spent most of their time in their trenches and went "over the top" into no-man's-land only at night, or during an attack. But there was a constant battle between soldiers in their facing lines of trenches. The opposing armies shot at anyone who was visible on the other side, even those trying to rescue the wounded from no-man's-land or retrieve the bodies of fallen soldiers. Raiding parties added to the danger. Every soldier was kept on full alert.

At close quarters

Soldiers carried a range of close-combat weapons when they went on raiding parties, in case they needed to kill an enemy silently, without being detected. Grenades were used to clear fortified enemy positions and firebays.

French trench knife

German stick grenade

German trench club

German Kugel (ball) grenade

British Mills bomb

Prepare to fire

These German troops on the Marne in 1914 are firing through loop holes. These enabled them to view and fire at the enemy without putting their heads above the parapet and exposing themselves to enemy fire. Later on in the war, sandbags replaced the earth ramparts.

Writing home

Both armies had chaplains and other clergy at the front. As a noncombatant, Canon Cyril Lomax had time to describe in illustrated letters home some of the horrors he encountered.

> ## "The German that I shot was a fine looking man... I did feel sorry but it was my life or his."
> —Jack Sweeney, British soldier, November 21, 1916

Walking wounded

This image shows wounded British soldiers returning from the front lines with a German prisoner (center). A soldier wounded in no-man's-land would be left until it was safe to bring him back to his trench, usually at nightfall. Some soldiers died because they could not be reached soon enough.

Path of bullet

Saved by a book

The soldier carrying this book was lucky. The pages slowed a bullet enough to minimize the injury it caused.

Always in action

These Bulgarian soldiers are eating their rations in a front line trench in Macedonia in 1916. Soldiers at the front had to be vigilant at all times, which is why their rifles are ready to be fired in case of attack, watched over by a sentry.

Field telephone

Most communication was by telephones relaying voice and Morse code messages.

Lines of
communication

To supply the vast and hungry armies along the Western Front, both sides put huge effort into lines of communication. The main form of transportation was the horse and, increasingly, motor vehicles. Germany made great use of railroads to move men and supplies to the front. Both sides set up elaborate supply systems to ensure that front line troops never ran out of ammunitions or food. Front line troops also kept in close touch with headquarters (HQ) and other units by telephone and wireless.

Getting in touch

Engineers, such as this German team, set up, maintained, and operated telephones in the field to ensure close and regular contact between the front line and HQ.

German message shell

Message rolled up in base

British night signal

Missile messages

Enemy fire often cut telephone lines, so both sides used shells to carry written messages. Signal grenades and rockets also sent prearranged messages to front line troops.

Pigeon post

Carrier pigeons were used to carry messages to and from the front line where telephone lines did not exist, although the birds often lost their way. Germany trained "war dogs" to carry messages in containers on their collars.

Canvas top secured with ropes

LOAD NOT TO
EXCEED 3 TONS

WD

Scale model of the British Wolseley 3 ton WD transport truck, built for war service

Two-way traffic

The lack of good roads to the front line meant that quiet country lanes suddenly became major thoroughfares. Columns of marching men, supply trucks, munitions wagons, field ambulances, and other vehicles moved in one direction while exhausted and wounded soldiers from the front line headed in the opposite direction.

Wounded British troops returning from the trenches in November 1916

Wheel power

Both sides built military trucks and vans to ferry men and supplies to the front line. Smaller, civilian vehicles were also used.

Fabulous baker girls

Behind the lines, vast quantities of food were produced every day to feed the soldiers at the front. British kitchens, canteens, and bakeries, such as this one, were often staffed by members of the Women's Army Auxiliary Corps (WAAC). Women also played a major role as clerks, telephone operators, and storekeepers, ensuring that the front line was adequately supplied and serviced at all times.

◉ EYEWITNESS

Margaret Caswell
One of the first WAAC servicewomen to be sent to the front in France was British volunteer Margaret Caswell (1896–1918). She joined the WAAC in 1917 at the age of 21 and worked as a waitress in the Abbeville camp. She was killed in an air raid in May 1918.

Keeping watch

Gathering intelligence about the enemy is vital to mounting a successful attack or repelling an enemy advance. As in every war, prisoners were interrogated. Nighttime patrols probed the strengths and weaknesses of enemy lines, crossing rows of barbed-wire entanglements and running the risk of attracting enemy gunfire. Aircraft flew overhead during the day, photographing the front line and observing details about the opposition, such as locations of their trenches and gun emplacements. This information was used to produce maps of enemy lines.

Aerial reconnaissance

Both sides used aircraft to observe enemy positions on the Western Front. At first, Allied commanders were suspicious of this new technology. But in September 1914, French Air Service pilots saw the advancing German armies change direction near Paris. This information helped the Allies to stop the German advance into France at the Battle of the Marne.

British Royal Aircraft Factory 1A V8 engine

Twin-seater cockpit

Canvas wing over wooden frame

Solid wheels

British Royal Aircraft Factory Blériot Experimental BE2c, an aircraft used for reconnaissance and light bombing

Compass bearings

A night patrol could get easily lost in no-man's-land, where any landmarks had all been blown away. A reflective compass was vital if the patrol was to navigate safely and get back to its own trench before daybreak.

Leather case

Mother-of-pearl face to catch the light

Glass front

Reconstruction of observation "tree," Imperial War Museum, London

Soldier rests on internal stepladder while looking through camouflaged spy hole

German stereoscopic periscope

Along the wire

The trenches were protected by rows of barbed-wire entanglements. Night patrols repaired the entanglements and—if an assault was planned for the next day—cleared a path through them for their infantry.

British double-strand barbed-wire

British wire cutters

German wire cutters

German single-strand barbed-wire

Loops to hang barbed-wire on

Screw secured picket in the ground

Silent posts

The first barbed-wire entanglements were strung along wooden posts knocked into the ground with mallets. When the hammering attracted enemy fire, both sides used metal pickets that were screwed silently into the ground.

Periscopes

Soldiers looking at the enemy over the top of a trench risked being shot at. To combat this, both sides used periscopes of varied types such as simple bayonet mirrors (below) and stereoscopic periscopes (left), which allowed them to peer over the trench parapet without being observed.

British soldier using bayonet mirror periscope

Bird's-eye view

Both sides used artificial trees as artillery observation posts to direct fire at the enemy. A soldier went up a ladder inside the tree and peered with binoculars at the enemy lines through a spy hole. He passed on what he saw to a soldier at the base of the post. The forward observation officer then relayed directions by telephone to an artillery battery behind the lines, so that it could aim its fire more accurately than before.

Bombardment

Artillery dominated the battlefields of World War I. A bombardment could destroy enemy trenches, knock out artillery batteries and communication lines, and help break up an infantry attack. As defenses strengthened, artillery bombardments became longer and more intense.

Sight saver

A chain-mail visor on British helmets made it hard to see and was soon removed.

German armor

In 1916, the German Army replaced its spiked *Pickelhauben* helmet (see p.13) with the *Stahlhelm*, a rounded, steel helmet, and issued body armor to machine gunners and sentries in trenches.

Stahlhelm (steel helmet)

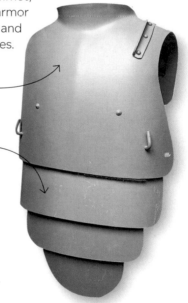

Breastplate

Articulated plates to cover lower body

Beware!

Soldiers at the front needed constant reminders to keep their heads down.

British 8-inch Mark V howitzer

Hiding the gun

Light field artillery was pulled by horses, while heavier guns, such as howitzers, were moved by tractors. Once in place, artillery pieces were camouflaged.

Shell power

A huge number of shells were needed to maintain a constant artillery barrage. In mid-1917, the British used a million shells a day. This munitions factory in Chilwell, England, filled more than half of all British shells with explosives during the war. Thousands of women and men worked in these factories across Britain. Munitions work was extremely dangerous, and people worked long hours.

Explosion!

In this dramatic picture, a French Renault tank comes under artillery fire in an attack. Tanks were obvious targets for field gunners, though most artillery fire was used to "soften up" the enemy before an attack.

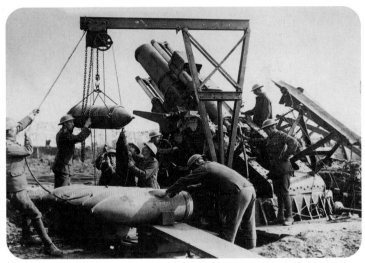

Loading a howitzer

Large pieces of artillery required a team of experienced gunners to load and fire them. This British 15-inch howitzer was used on the Menin Road near Ypres, Belgium, in October 1917. Its huge, heavy shell is being winched into position.

British 13-pounder shrapnel shell	French 75-mm shrapnel shell	British 4.5-inch high-explosive shell	German 15-cm shrapnel shell

Artillery shells

High-explosive shells exploded on impact. Anti-personnel shrapnel shells exploded in flight as they were designed to kill or maim people, not destroy buildings or vehicles.

Over the top

Once the artillery bombardment had pounded the enemy's defenses, the infantry climbed out of their trenches and advanced toward enemy lines. But bombardments rarely knocked out all enemy defenses, and gaps were often covered by machine-gun crews. A soldier armed with only a rifle and bayonet and laden with heavy equipment was an easy target.

Leaving the trench

The most frightening moment for a soldier was climbing out of his trench and into no-man's-land. This painting by British painter John Nash depicts soldiers of the 1st Artists' Rifles going "over the top" in 1917.

In action

This German machine-gun crew protects the flank (side) of advancing infantry. The maneuverability, reliability, and firepower of machine guns made them effective weapons, though they were vulnerable to well-aimed artillery.

Water-cooled barrel

Tripod mounting

British 0.303 in Maxim Mark III medium machine gun

EYEWITNESS

Ernest Brooks

British photographer Ernest Brooks (1876–1957) was the first official photographer of the British Army. He took the first British official photographs of World War I, such as the photograph of the wounded soldier (far right) at Thiepval, France, during the Battle of the Somme.

Quick firing

Machine guns fired up to 600 bullets a minute. Ammunition was fitted into a belt, or in a tray fed into the gun automatically.

Months in the mud

The Battle of the Somme in France lasted from July 1, 1916, until November 18, when snow and rain brought the attack to a muddy halt. The Allies took about 48 sq miles (125 sq km) of land but failed to break through the German lines north of the Somme River.

Tending the wounded

The cramped conditions of a communication trench can be seen in this image (taken by Ernest Brooks) of an army medical orderly tending a wounded soldier at Thiepval near the Somme in September 1916.

> **"The sunken road...(was)... filled with pieces of uniform, weapons, and dead bodies."**
> —*Lieutenant Ernst Jünger, German soldier, the Somme, 1916*

First day of the Somme

The British began a six-day artillery bombardment on June 24, but the Germans retreated into deep bunkers and were largely unharmed. As the British infantry advanced at 7:30 a.m. on July 1, German machine gunners opened fire. On that first day alone, they killed or injured two British soldiers along every 3 ft (1 m) of the 16-mile (25-km) front.

Soldiers of the 103rd (Tyneside Irish) Brigade attack La Boisselle on the first day of the Somme.

Wounded

An estimated 21 million soldiers were wounded in the war. Caring for them was a major military operation. Wounded soldiers were first treated in the trenches, then moved to casualty clearing stations behind the front line for proper medical attention, then on to base hospitals still further from the front. Soldiers with severe injuries were sent home to recover in hospitals.

Lucky wound

When a splinter from a shell pierced his helmet, this soldier escaped with only a minor head wound. Many men hoped for injuries that were not too serious but that would send them home. British soldiers called them "Blighty wounds"—Blighty being a slang word for Britain.

Bottles of liquid antiseptics and painkillers

Inventory listing contents and where to find them in the pouch

The German kit

German medical orderlies carried two first-aid pouches on their belts. One contained basic antiseptics and painkillers, while the other contained dressings and triangular bandages.

Trench aid

Injured soldiers had their wounds dressed by medical orderlies in the trench where they fell, before being taken to an aid post for assessment.

Strip of lace curtain

German bandages

Recycled bandages

Following the naval blockade by Britain, Germany ran out of cotton and linen. Wood fiber, paper, and lace curtains were used to make bandages.

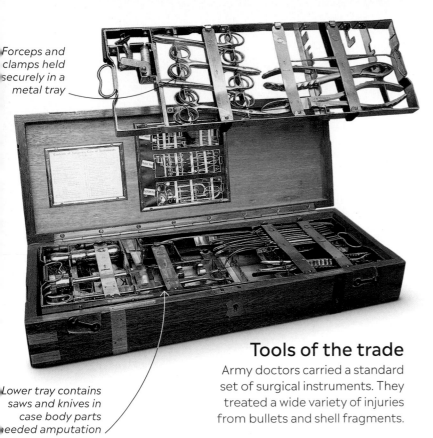

Forceps and clamps held securely in a metal tray

Lower tray contains saws and knives in case body parts needed amputation

Tools of the trade

Army doctors carried a standard set of surgical instruments. They treated a wide variety of injuries from bullets and shell fragments.

The field hospital

Farmhouses, ruined factories, and even bombed-out churches were used as casualty clearing stations to treat the wounded.

Shellshock

Shell shock—the collective term for concussion, emotional shock, nervous exhaustion, and similar ailments—was not identified before World War I, but trench warfare was so horrific that large numbers of soldiers developed symptoms. For some, shell shock was almost immediate. Most eventually recovered, but some suffered nightmares and other effects on their mental health. Today, medical experts understand that it also had longer-term effects, such as post-traumatic stress disorder (PTSD).

Red Cross symbol to signify non-combatant status of the ambulance

Wounded men were often in a state of shock.

Bunks for the injured to lie on

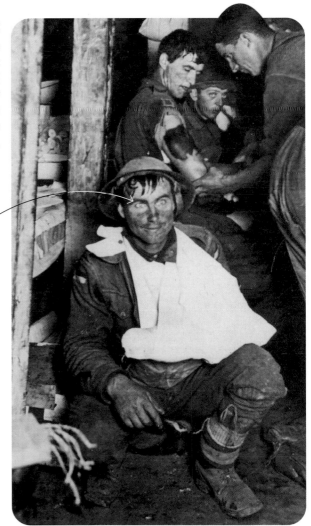

Ambulance

The British Royal Army Medical Corps, like its German counterpart, used field ambulances to carry the wounded to the hospital. Many ambulances were staffed by volunteers, including women.

Wounded British soldiers at a dressing station near Ypres

Women at war

With so many men fighting, there was a shortage of workers at home. Many women were already in work but were restricted to domestic labor, nursing, teaching, or working on the family farm—jobs then considered suitable for women. Now they went to work in factories, drove trucks and ambulances, and did almost everything that only men had done before. When the war ended, most women were expected to return to their domestic duties at home.

This Russian poster from 1916 shows a female factory worker.

Support your country

Images of women taking up jobs usually held by men were used to gain support for a country's war effort. This Russian poster urges people to buy war bonds (loans to the government).

Women's Army Auxiliary Corps

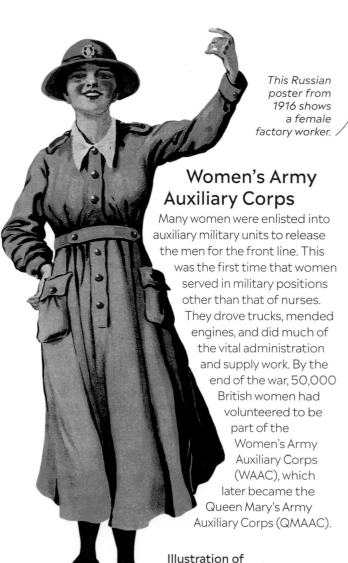

Many women were enlisted into auxiliary military units to release the men for the front line. This was the first time that women served in military positions other than that of nurses. They drove trucks, mended engines, and did much of the vital administration and supply work. By the end of the war, 50,000 British women had volunteered to be part of the Women's Army Auxiliary Corps (WAAC), which later became the Queen Mary's Army Auxiliary Corps (QMAAC).

Illustration of QMAAC volunteer

👁 EYEWITNESS

Elsie Knocker

British nurse and ambulance driver Elsie Knocker (1884–1978) served during World War I. She and her friend Mairi Chisholm (below, right) set up a nursing station immediately behind the front line for dressing the wounded. They were injured in a gas attack in 1918 and had to return home.

Women's Land Army
The war required a huge increase in food production at home as both sides tried to restrict the enemy's imports of food from abroad. Millions of women already worked the land across Europe, however, Britain saw a shortage of farm workers. In February 1917, the Women's Land Army was set up in Britain, and 113,000 women joined up to provide a well-paid workforce for farms.

Working in poverty
The war brought increased status and wealth to many women, but not all. In factories across Italy (above), Germany, and Russia, women worked long, hard hours but earned barely enough to feed their families. Strikes led by women were very common as a result.

Letters to men at the front describing events at home

Mementos from home
Women wrote letters to their husbands, brothers, and sons at the front. They often enclosed keepsakes, such as photographs or pressed flowers, to remind them of home. These did much to raise the morale of homesick and often very frightened troops. Men also sent home personal souvenirs, like this embroidered lace handkerchief.

Lace handkerchief

Leather face mask

Cowl type flying helmet

Anti-splinter glass goggles

War in the air

Turned-up collar to keep neck warm

When war broke out in 1914, powered flight was barely 10 years old. The first warplanes flew as reconnaissance craft, looking down on enemy lines or helping to direct artillery fire. Enemy pilots tried to shoot them down, leading to dogfights in the sky between highly skilled and brave "aces." Specialized fighter planes were soon produced by both sides, as were sturdier craft capable of carrying bombs.

Coat of soft, supple leather

Sheepskin-lined leather gloves to protect against frostbite

Sopwith Camel

The Sopwith F1 Camel first flew in battle in June 1917 and became the most successful Allied fighter in shooting down German aircraft.

Dressed for the air

Pilots flew in open cockpits, so they wore leather coats, balaclavas, and boots and gloves lined with sheepskin to keep out the cold. One-piece suits also became common.

Sheepskin boots

Thick sole to give a good grip

Captain René Fonck (1894–1953), France—75 victories

Rittmeister Manfred von Richthofen (1892–1918), center, Germany—80 victories

British 20 lb Hales bomb, containing 4.5 lb (2 kg) of explosives

British Carcass incendiary bomb

Bombs away

At first, bombs were dropped over the side of the aircraft by the pilot. Soon, specialized bomber aircraft were fitted with bombsights, bomb racks under the fuselage, and release systems.

Captain Albert Ball (1896–1917), Britain—44 victories

Air aces

To qualify as an air "ace," a pilot had to bring down at least five enemy aircraft. Baron von Richthofen—the "Red Baron"—was the highest-scoring ace of the war, shooting down 80 Allied aircraft. Britain's ace pilot Captain Albert Ball was only 20 when he was shot down and killed in 1917.

Captain Eddie Rickenbacker (1890–1973), US—26 victories

Fokker D.VII

German fighter

The German Fokker D.VII appeared in April 1918. Although slower than the Sopwith Camel, it climbed rapidly and flew well at all altitudes.

BMW engine

Side cutaway to show internal steel-tubing framework

Maneuvers

The art of aerial warfare was unknown to pilots at the start of the war. This British instruction poster shows the correct method of attacking a German fighter.

German aircraft holds a steady course

British fighter comes up from below and behind

Wooden struts

Wooden, box-structure wings covered with canvas

26.9 ft (8.2 m) wingspan

Symbol of British Royal Flying Corps, later the Royal Air Force

"You ask me to 'let the devils have it'... when I fight... I don't think them devils... I only scrap because it is my duty."
—Captain Albert Ball, 1916

The gun fired a shell known as a "1-pounder common shell", which weighed 1 lb (0.45 kg).

Hardit Singh Malik

Known as the Flying Sikh, Hardit Singh Malik (1894–1985) was the first Indian pilot of World War I. He joined the British Royal Flying Corps in 1917. Hardit was wounded while hunting the "Red Baron" during the Third Battle of Ypres.

Anti-aircraft guns

Early anti-aircraft guns, such as this British QF 1-pounder, fired from ships at torpedo boats. Once adapted for high-angle shooting, they could hit aircraft from dry land.

Pivot to change direction and angle of gun

Zeppelin

The first airship was designed by the German Count Ferdinand von Zeppelin in 1900. Early in the war, airships could fly higher than planes, so it was almost impossible to shoot them down. This made them useful for carrying out bombing raids. But higher flying aircraft and the use of incendiary (fire-making) bullets soon brought these aerial bombers down to earth. By 1917, most German and British airships were restricted to reconnaissance work at sea.

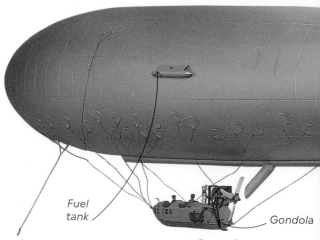

Fuel tank　　*Gondola*

Sea Scout Zero

Britain's SSZ (Sea Scout Zero) was a nonrigid airship with no internal framework. It was light, had a top speed of 45 mph (72 km/h), and could stay airborne for 17 hours. It was employed mainly on submarine patrol or on escort duty for convoys.

German incendiary bomb dropped by Zeppelin LZ 38 on London, May 31, 1915

Inside the gondola

Exposed to the weather, the crew operated the airship from the open-sided gondola—a cabin below the main airship.

Bombing runs

Crews in the first airships had to drop their bombs over the side of the gondola by hand. Later models had automatic release mechanisms.

Getting bigger

This L3 German airship took part in the first airship raid on Britain on the night of January 19–20, 1915, causing 20 civilian casualties and enormous panic.

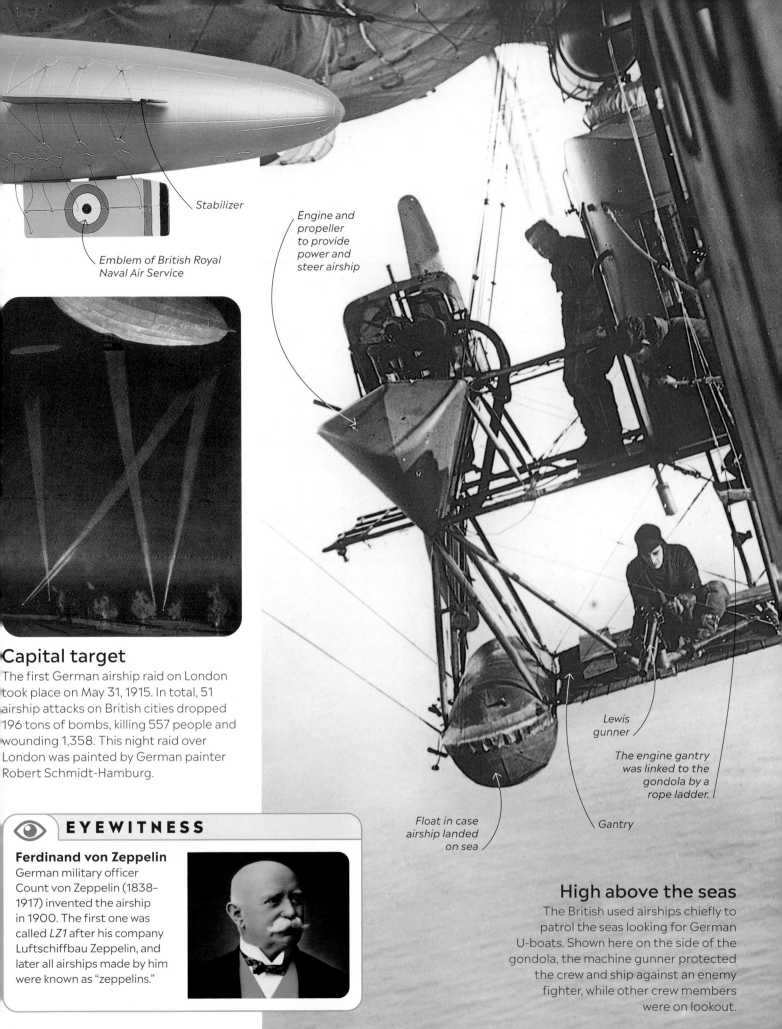

Stabilizer

Emblem of British Royal Naval Air Service

Engine and propeller to provide power and steer airship

Capital target

The first German airship raid on London took place on May 31, 1915. In total, 51 airship attacks on British cities dropped 196 tons of bombs, killing 557 people and wounding 1,358. This night raid over London was painted by German painter Robert Schmidt-Hamburg.

Lewis gunner

The engine gantry was linked to the gondola by a rope ladder.

Gantry

Float in case airship landed on sea

Ferdinand von Zeppelin
German military officer Count von Zeppelin (1838–1917) invented the airship in 1900. The first one was called *LZ1* after his company Luftschiffbau Zeppelin, and later all airships made by him were known as "zeppelins."

High above the seas

The British used airships chiefly to patrol the seas looking for German U-boats. Shown here on the side of the gondola, the machine gunner protected the crew and ship against an enemy fighter, while other crew members were on lookout.

War **at sea**

The war at sea was a grueling one. Fleet battles were rare, but there were many smaller engagements that took their toll. For its part, the British Royal Navy maintained an effective blockade, keeping supplies from reaching German ports. In return, the Germans waged a submarine U-boat war against Allied ships that were bringing food and other vital supplies to Britain.

Life inside a U-boat

Conditions inside a U-boat were cramped, and fumes and heat from the engine made the air very stuffy. The crew had to navigate their craft through minefields and avoid detection in order to attack enemy ships.

Constant threat

This German poster, *The U-boats are out!,* shows the threat posed to Allied shipping by the German U-boat fleet.

Land and sea

Seaplanes can take off and land on both water and the ground. Used for reconnaissance and bombing, they could sink an enemy ship with a torpedo.

Floats for landing on water

Observation balloon

Gun

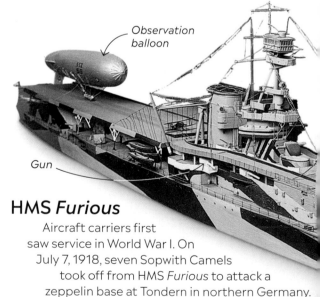

HMS *Furious*

Aircraft carriers first saw service in World War I. On July 7, 1918, seven Sopwith Camels took off from HMS *Furious* to attack a zeppelin base at Tondern in northern Germany.

Success and failure

German U-boats operated under the sea and on the surface. Here, a deck cannon fires at an enemy steamer. The U-boats sank 5,554 Allied and neutral merchant ships as well as many warships. But 178 of the 372 U-boats were destroyed by Allied guns, bombs, sea mines, or torpedoes.

Dazzled

Many artists contributed to their country's war effort, some in surprising ways. The British painter Edward Wadsworth supervised the application of "dazzle" camouflage to ships' hulls. In 1919, he painted the picture above, *Dazzle ships in dry dock at Liverpool,* showing the finished result.

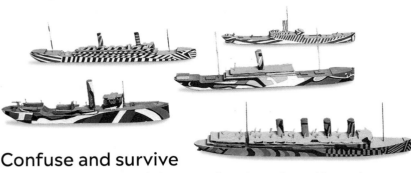

Confuse and survive

From 1917, the British Admiralty camouflaged merchant ships and their escorts with gray, black, and blue geometric patterns. This distorted the silhouette of the ship and made it difficult for German U-boats to target.

Brave sailor

British sailor John Cornwell was only 16 when his ship came under heavy fire during the Battle of Jutland. He was gravely wounded, but stayed at his post till the end of the battle, later dying of his wounds. He was awarded the Victoria Cross posthumously for his bravery. While originally thought to be him, it is now believed this picture may be of his brother.

Battle of Jutland

Britain's Royal Navy was the biggest in the world and followed the "two-power standard"—its might equaled that of the two next strongest nations combined. At the Battle of Jutland (May 31—June 1, 1916), when the British Grand Fleet met the German High Seas Fleet, 14 British and 11 German ships were lost. However, while both sides proclaimed victory, it was British naval power that remained dominant. This image (right) shows Royal Navy ships of the Grand Fleet sailing in Line Ahead formation, which allowed them to fire their guns when needed.

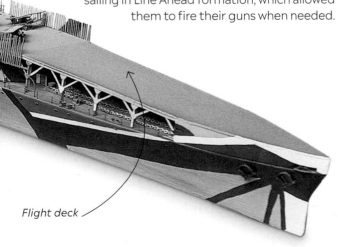

Flight deck

Gallipoli

In March 1915, the Allies tried to force through the Dardanelles Strait by naval power alone to threaten the Ottoman Turkish capital, Constantinople. The attacks failed. A month later, on April 25, British, French, and Anzac troops landed at Gallipoli, and were held close to the beaches by the Ottomans. In August, a second Allied landing at Suvla Bay amounted to nothing, as they faced a fierce Turkish resistance. The death rate mounted, and the Allies eventually withdrew in January 1916.

Tasty greetings
A British Army biscuit was so hard, a soldier in Gallipoli wrote this Christmas card on it.

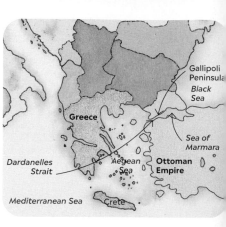

Gallipoli Peninsula
The Gallipoli Peninsula lies to the north of the Dardanelles Strait. Britain and France wanted direct access from the Mediterranean to the Black Sea and their ally, Russia. But the narrow waterway was controlled by Germany's ally, the Ottoman Empire.

Dugout camps

No part was safe from Turkish fire

Anzac Cove
The Australian and New Zealand Army Corps, known as the Anzacs, landed on the western coast of the Gallipoli Peninsula. The narrow beach and steep, sandy hills gave the men little cover from Turkish fire. Around 11,000 Anzacs died at Gallipoli. Australia and New Zealand both remember their war dead on Anzac Day, April 25.

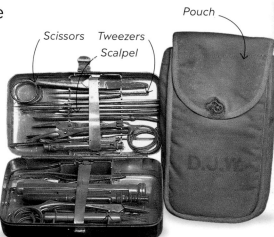

Scissors *Tweezers* *Scalpel* *Pouch*

Hypodermic needles

Privately purchased medical gear used by a British officer on the front line

The casualty rate
The treatment and evacuation of casualties from Gallipoli was complicated by the huge numbers of sick soldiers as well as those who were wounded.

German help
To the Allies' surprise, Gallipoli was strongly defended by Turkish trenches, barbed-wire entanglements, and artillery. Germany also equipped the Turks with modern pistols, rifles, machine guns, and artillery.

Improvised grenades
The fighting at Gallipoli was often at very close range. In a munitions shortage, Allied troops used jam tins to make hand-thrown grenades.

The sick beach

On both sides, food was contaminated by flies carrying disease from the many corpses. Dysentery was rife—most of the Anzac troops in a hospital at Anzac Cove (below) had it.

Jetty for boats carrying sick and wounded soldiers

Winter evacuation

When the Allies decided to withdraw from Gallipoli, a flotilla of ships evacuated the troops and their supplies. Unlike the chaos and carnage of the previous six months, the withdrawals under the cover of darkness went without a hitch and not one man was injured

Ottoman sultan's cypher (seal) with the year 1333 in the Muslim calendar, which is 1915 in the Western calendar

For distinction

Created in 1915, the Turkish War Medal, also known as the Gallipoli Star, was awarded to German and Turkish soldiers who fought at Gallipoli.

British troops evacuate on rafts from Suvla Bay, December 1915.

Verdun

On February 21, 1916, Germany launched a massive attack against Verdun, a fortified French city. Close to the German border, Verdun controlled access into eastern France. After a huge, eight-hour artillery bombardment, the German infantry advanced. The French were caught by surprise but held out. By December, the Germans had been pushed back almost to where they started. The human cost was enormous—some 377,000 French and 337,000 German soldiers were killed or wounded in the battle.

War poster

During the battle of Verdun, French general Philippe Pétain rallied his soldiers with the war cry *"On les aura!"* ("We'll get them!"). The French painter Jules Abel Faivre adopted the phrase to create the poster above. It was used to appeal to businesses and investors to donate money to the government for the war effort.

Les poilus

The French infantry were nicknamed *les poilus*, or "the hairy ones," because of their hairy beards and mustaches. These soldiers bore the brunt of the German attack. Cold, muddy, and wet, they suffered dreadful injuries from shellfire and gas.

Machine-gun post

Exposed concrete fort wall

Fort Douaumont

Verdun was protected by three rings of fortifications. Fort Douaumont, in the outer ring, was the largest of these forts. Defended by just 56 elderly reservists, it fell to the Germans on February 25.

Ruined cityscape

On February 25, the historic city of Verdun was evacuated. Many buildings were hit by the artillery bombardment, and even more were destroyed by fires that often raged for days.

At close quarters

Fighting at Verdun was fierce, as both sides repeatedly attacked and counterattacked the same forts and strategic areas around the city. Advancing attackers were mowed down by artillery bombardment or machine-gun fire from inside the forts. The open ground was too exposed for rescuers to retrieve the dead, and bodies were left to rot. This photograph is from the 1928 movie *Verdun, visions d'histoire*, by Léon Poirier, which is one of the many dramatic movies made about the war.

> ## "What a bloodbath, what horrid images, what a slaughter. I just cannot find the words to express my feelings. Hell cannot be this dreadful."
> —Albert Joubaire, French soldier, Verdun, 1916

Légion d'Honneur

In tribute to the people of Verdun's suffering, the French president awarded the *Légion d'Honneur* to the city. It is usually given for individual acts of bravery.

Laurel-leaf wreath, symbol of triumph

Oak-leaf wreath, symbol of wisdom

Head of Marianne, symbol of France

A muddy wasteland

The land around Verdun is wooded and hilly, with many streams running down to the Meuse River. Heavy rainfall and constant artillery bombardment turned it into a desolate mud bath, where the dead lay half buried in shell craters and the living had to eat and sleep within inches of fallen comrades. This photograph shows the "Ravin de la mort," the Ravine of Death.

Gas attack

On April 22, 1915, French Algerian troops near the Belgian town of Ypres noticed a greenish-yellow cloud moving toward them from the German front line. The cloud was chlorine gas. This was the first time poison gas had been used effectively in war, and the troops had no protection against its choking effects. Over the next three years, new gases and gas tactics were used, leaving 91,000 dead from their effects.

British "Hypo" helmet

Early warning

The first anti-gas masks were crude and ineffective. Basic goggles protected the eyes, and mouth pads made of cloth were soaked in chemicals to neutralize the gas.

British anti-gas goggles

Flannel respirator

British small box respirator

Black veil respirator

Hand shrunk

When exposed to some kinds of gas, a leather glove will shrink. This is what happens to a person's lungs when exposed to the same gas.

Glove shrunken by gas

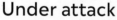

Ordinary glove

All-in-one

By the middle of the war, both sides wore protective helmets fitted with face masks, goggles, and respirators. These shielded the eyes, nose, and throat from the potentially lethal effects of gas. Gas alarms, such as whistles (right), horns, and gongs, helped give warning of an incoming gas attack.

Gas alarm whistle

Under attack

The first effects of gas were felt on the face and in the eyes, but within seconds it entered the throat. Soldiers coughed and choked as the gas swirled around them. The long-term effects depended on the type of gas used—some soldiers died very quickly; others were blinded for life or suffered awful blisters or died a lingering death as their lungs collapsed and filled with liquid. This photograph shows US troops in a staged gas attack and was used for training new recruits.

Gassed

In *Gassed*, a 1919 painting from life by the American war artist John Singer Sargent, blinded soldiers are led by sighted colleagues toward a dressing station near Arras in northern France in August 1918.

Animal welfare

Every living creature was vulnerable to gas, including the many thousands of horses used by both sides to transport men, equipment, and supplies. This German rider and horse both wear gas masks.

German gas mask

Eyes not protected

Canvas-covered respirator

GERMAN GAS SHELLS

German gas shells contained liquid gas, which evaporated into the air on impact. Several types of gas were used. Dichloroethyl sulfide, known as "Mustard gas," burned the skin, caused temporary blindness, and, if inhaled, flooded the lungs and led to death from pneumonia. Diphenylchloroarsine ("Sneezing oil") brought on violent sneezing, forcing soldiers to remove their masks. All sides used gas shells to attack the enemy.

Phosgene & diphosgene

Diphosgene

Tear gas (Lachrymatory)

Diphosgene and diphenylchloroarsine ("Sneezing oil")

Mustard gas

In the east

After the failure of the assault in the west in 1914, the Germans went on the defensive. The Western Front became locked in trench warfare, while attention turned to the east. Here the armies of Germany and Austria-Hungary fought the Russians over vast swathes of territory. The Russians were often badly led and poorly equipped, and suffered huge losses. By 1916, the German Army was in full control of the entire Eastern Front.

Tannenberg, 1914

In August 1914, Russia's First and Second armies invaded East Prussia, Germany. The Second Army was surrounded at Tannenberg and forced to surrender on August 31, with the loss of 150,000 men and most of its artillery.

German troops in trenches

Masurian Lakes, 1914

In September 1914, the Russian First Army had marched to the Masurian Lakes in East Prussia and found itself in danger of being surrounded. German troops dug trenches and other defenses and attacked the Russians, who soon withdrew, sustaining more than 100,000 casualties. By the end of September, the Russian threat to Germany was over.

Siege of Przemyśl

Przemyśl was an Austro-Hungarian fortress in Galicia that was besieged by Russian troops in November 1914, and fell 181 days later in March 1915. Here, Russian troops are marching to defend the newly captured city.

Maria Bochkareva
In 1914, Russian soldier Maria Bochkareva (1889–1920) petitioned for women to be enlisted as fighters in the war. It worked, and in May 1917, she proposed all-women battalions to fight for the cause. She was wounded in the Kerensky Offensive of July 1917.

Unwilling to fight

By the end of 1916, many Russian soldiers were refusing to fight. Starving and badly treated, they saw little reason to risk their lives in a war they did not believe in. Such low morale led, in part, to the Russian Revolution of 1917.

The Italian Front

On May 23, 1915, Italy joined the war on the side of the Allies and prepared to invade its hostile neighbor, Austria-Hungary. Fighting took place on two fronts, to Italy's north and east. The Italian Army was ill prepared and underequipped for the war and was unable to break through Austrian defenses until its final success at the Battle of Vittorio Veneto in October 1918.

The Isonzo River

The Isonzo flowed between the mountains of Austria-Hungary and the plains of northeast Italy. After 11 battles along the river, victory fell to the Austrians, with German support, at Caporetto in 1917.

Italian alpinists
Most of the 400-mile (640 km) Italian frontier with Austria-Hungary lay in the Italian Alps. Both sides used trained alpine troops to fight in mountainous terrain.

War in the desert

World War I was not restricted to Europe. A major conflict took place in the Middle East, which was largely controlled by the Turkish Ottoman Empire. The British invaded Mesopotamia (now Iraq) in 1914 but were defeated by the Ottomans at Kut-al-Amara. British and Indian troops finally recaptured the town in 1917. A British force, under General Allenby, captured Palestine and the Syrian capital of Damascus. In Arabia, Bedouin soldiers under the guidance of T. E. Lawrence rose in revolt against Turkish rule.

Fighting in Palestine

In 1917, Britain opened a new front against Ottoman Turkey. British troops of the Egyptian Expeditionary Force (EEF) under General Allenby won the Third Battle of Gaza in November and captured Jerusalem in December. British and Arab armies captured Damascus on October 1, 1918. Ottoman Turkey surrendered within a month.

Lawrence of Arabia

British soldier T. E. Lawrence became the legendary figure known as Lawrence of Arabia. As liaison officer to Emir Feisal, leader of the Arab revolt against Ottoman Turkish rule, Lawrence helped the Arabs to become an effective guerrilla force. They blew up railroad lines, attacked garrisons, and tied down an army many times their own size.

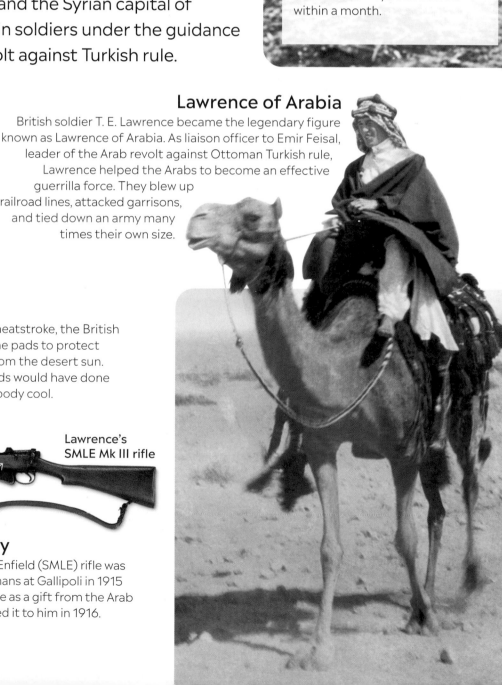

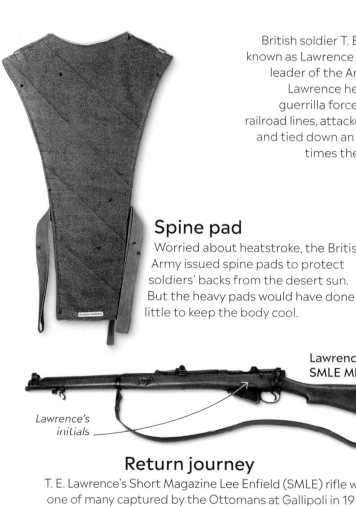

Spine pad

Worried about heatstroke, the British Army issued spine pads to protect soldiers' backs from the desert sun. But the heavy pads would have done little to keep the body cool.

Lawrence's SMLE Mk III rifle

Lawrence's initials

Return journey

T. E. Lawrence's Short Magazine Lee Enfield (SMLE) rifle was one of many captured by the Ottomans at Gallipoli in 1915 (see p.40). It found its way to Lawrence as a gift from the Arab leader, Emir Feisal, who presented it to him in 1916.

Ottoman troops in Jerusalem, 1917

Sand shoes

Walking across sand is tiring. These British wire sand shoes were worn over the soldier's boots, to spread his weight, so he did not sink in the sand.

Leather loop

Webbing strap

Signpost from a crossroads in Jerusalem

JERICHO Rᴅ.
ᴛᴏ DAMASCUS Gᵀᴱ
& NABLUS ROAD.

ᵀᴏ JAFFA Gᵀᴱ
STATION &
HEBRON Rᴅ

March to Baghdad

In November 1914, Britain sent troops to Mesopotamia, which was rich in the oil that fueled its navy. In April 1916, after a long siege, British and Indian troops at Kut-al-Amara were forced to surrender to Ottoman troops (seen here crossing a pontoon bridge in Baghdad). Around 13,000 British and Indian troops were captured. This major defeat was finally overturned by the British when they captured Baghdad in March 1917.

German sign celebrating the fall of the Kut

Interesting War News of April 29ᵗʰ 1916 Kut el Amara has been taken by the Turcs and the whole english army their 13 000 men maken prisoners.

Espionage

Both sides suspected the other of employing hundreds of spies in enemy territory, but most espionage work consisted of eavesdropping on enemy communications. Code-breaking, or cryptography, was crucial, as both sides sent and received coded messages by radio and telegraph. Cryptographers devised complex codes to ensure the safe transit of their own messages while using their skills to intercept and break coded enemy messages.

Lightweight, but strong, string attaches parachute to bird

Corset made of linen and padded to protect bird

Pigeon post

More than 100,000 pigeons were used to carry messages between intelligence agents and their home bases. The pigeons were dropped by parachute into occupied areas and collected by agents. Messages were attached to their legs, and they were released to fly back to their lofts.

Reading the enemy

Army intelligence officers, such as this British soldier, played a vital role in examining and understanding captured enemy documents. They pieced together information about enemy plans or morale, and sent it to the military high command.

Seized German documents being analyzed

Secret ink

Special ink was used to write invisible messages on paper. The message could be read later when treated with a chemical to make the words visible.

German invisible ink

Invisible-ink bottle

Edith Cavell

British nurse Edith Cavell (1865–1915) ran a nursing school in Brussels, Belgium, where she helped wounded Allied soldiers escape from the German-occupied country—sometimes with German secrets. Arrested and found guilty of "war treason," Cavell was shot in 1915.

Front of button

Button message

Tiny and unobtrusive, coded messages were stamped on to the back of buttons sewn on to coats or jackets.

Coded message on back of button

Hidden messages

Two Dutch agents sent to England to spy for Germany pretended to be cigar importers. They used their cigar orders as codes for the ships they observed in Portsmouth Harbour. In 1915, they were caught and executed.

Cigars slit open in search of hidden messages

Matchbox

Aid to escape

This food can was sent to British Lieutenant Jack Shaw at a German prisoner-of-war camp in 1918. It contained maps, wire cutters, and compasses for a mass escape.

Lead weights to make the can the correct weight

Rolled-up map of France

Compass

Lens cap

Camera lens

Pocket camera

This miniature camera disguised as a fob watch was used to take secret photographs in German East Africa (now Tanzania).

Shutter release

Mata Hari

Dutch-born Margaretha Zelle was a famous dancer who used the stage name Mata Hari. She had many high-ranking lovers, who revealed confidential information, which she passed to the French secret service. When fed false information by a German diplomat, she was shot as a German spy by the French in 1917.

Tank warfare

The invention of the tank changed warfare forever. Originating in Britain, the machine was a mobile armed fort designed to flatten barbed-wire, cross enemy trenches, and shield the advancing infantry. First used during the Battle of the Somme in 1916, it was at the Battle of Cambrai in November 1917 that the use of massed tanks first displayed its full potential. They played a vital role at the Battle of Amiens on August 8, 1918, and helped deliver victory in the final Allied advances.

Stabilizer wheels

Equipped with two six-pounder guns and four machine guns

British Mark I tank

The first tank to see action was the British Mark I tank. Of the 49 built for the Battle of the Somme on September 15, 1916, only 15 went into battle. They were not alone as the French developed their own tanks, first used on April 16, 1917.

Protect and survive

British tank crews wore leather helmets with visors and chain mail mouthpieces to protect their heads against specks of hot metal that flew off the inside of the hull when the tank was hit by bullets.

A7V tank

In 1918, too late to make any real impact, the Germans built the huge A7V, a 73,855 lb (33,500 kg) tank with six machine guns and a crew of 18. Only 20 A7Vs were constructed.

German A7V tank

British Mark V tank

Inside a tank

The tank was hot, noisy, fume-ridden, and badly ventilated, making the crew sick or even faint. The engine was so hot that there was danger of fire, and bullets hitting the tank produced dangerous shards of metal.

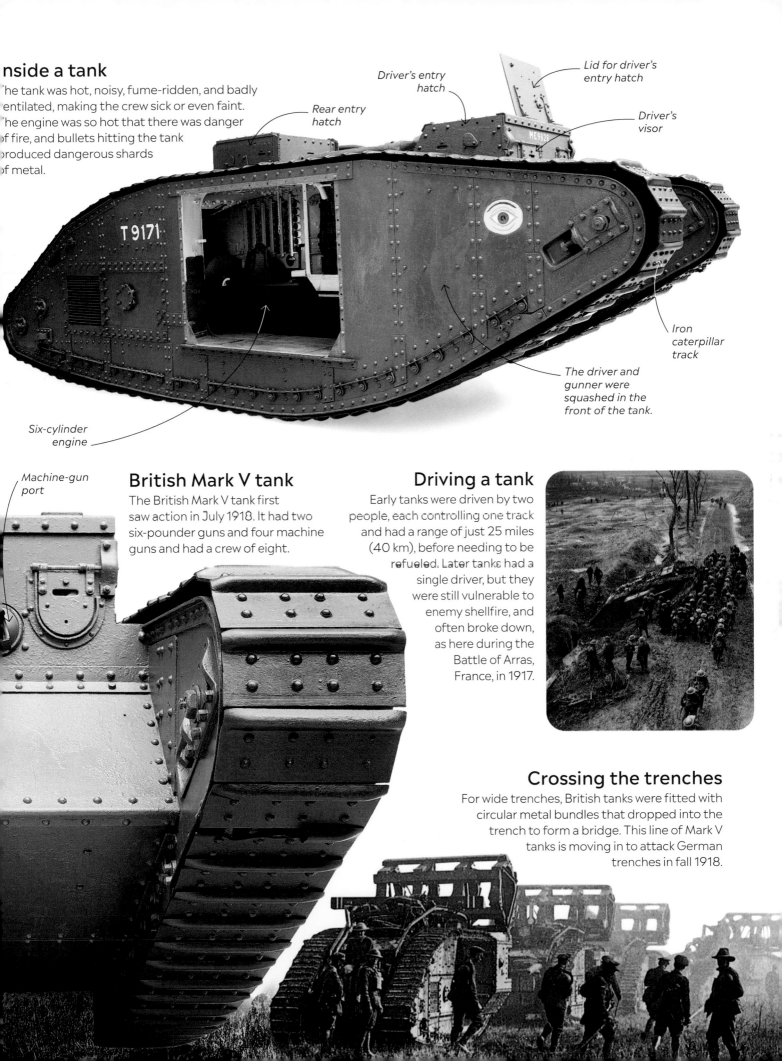

Driver's entry hatch

Lid for driver's entry hatch

Rear entry hatch

Driver's visor

ME9624

T 9171

Iron caterpillar track

The driver and gunner were squashed in the front of the tank.

Six-cylinder engine

Machine-gun port

British Mark V tank

The British Mark V tank first saw action in July 1918. It had two six-pounder guns and four machine guns and had a crew of eight.

Driving a tank

Early tanks were driven by two people, each controlling one track and had a range of just 25 miles (40 km), before needing to be refueled. Later tanks had a single driver, but they were still vulnerable to enemy shellfire, and often broke down, as here during the Battle of Arras, France, in 1917.

Crossing the trenches

For wide trenches, British tanks were fitted with circular metal bundles that dropped into the trench to form a bridge. This line of Mark V tanks is moving in to attack German trenches in fall 1918.

The US joins in

When war broke out in Europe in 1914, the US remained neutral. In 1917, Germany decided to attack all foreign shipping to try to limit supplies to Britain. It also tried to divert US attention from Europe by encouraging its neighbor Mexico to invade. This action outraged the US government, and as more US ships were sunk, President Woodrow Wilson declared war on Germany. This was a major blow to the Central Powers.

Uncle Sam

The all-American figure of Uncle Sam was used in a US recruiting poster based on Kitchener's British original (see p.14). Beneath his pointing finger were the words "I WANT YOU FOR THE US ARMY."

Lifebelt salvaged from the RMS Lusitania

RMS Lusitania

On May 7, 1915, the passenger ship RMS Lusitania was sunk off the Irish coast by German torpedoes, for allegedly carrying munitions. The victims included 128 US citizens. Their death did much to turn the US public against Germany and toward the Allies.

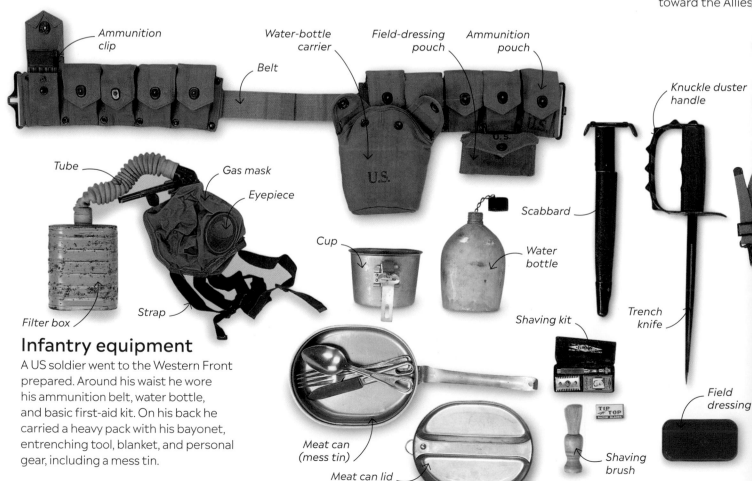

Ammunition clip · Water-bottle carrier · Field-dressing pouch · Ammunition pouch · Belt · Knuckle duster handle · Tube · Gas mask · Eyepiece · Scabbard · Cup · Water bottle · Strap · Filter box · Shaving kit · Trench knife · Meat can (mess tin) · Meat can lid · Shaving brush · Field dressing

Infantry equipment

A US soldier went to the Western Front prepared. Around his waist he wore his ammunition belt, water bottle, and basic first-aid kit. On his back he carried a heavy pack with his bayonet, entrenching tool, blanket, and personal gear, including a mess tin.

Gun fire

The US First Army first saw major action in September 1918 at St. Mihiel, south of Verdun, France, in an Allied attack on German lines. Here an artillery crew fires a field gun, surrounded by shell cases.

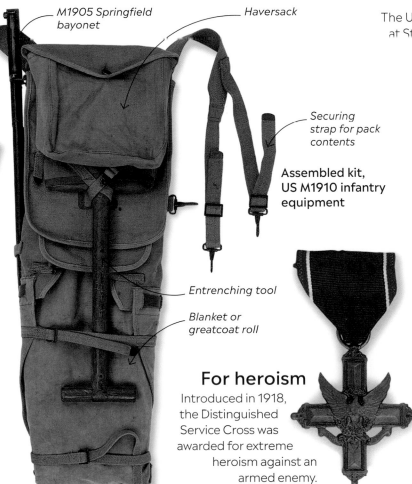

M1905 Springfield bayonet

Haversack

Securing strap for pack contents

Assembled kit, US M1910 infantry equipment

Entrenching tool

Blanket or greatcoat roll

For heroism

Introduced in 1918, the Distinguished Service Cross was awarded for extreme heroism against an armed enemy.

👁 **EYEWITNESS**

Kathryn M. Johnson

Black US political activist Kathryn M. Johnson (1878–1954), along with fellow activist Addie W. Hunton (below, right), were sent by the Young Men's Christian Association (YMCA) to France to observe how Black soldiers were treated by the US Army in segregated units. On their return, Johnson and Hunton co-wrote about the discrimination faced by Black US soldiers in their book *Two Colored Women with the American Expeditionary Forces*.

Mines and **mud**

For much of the war on the Western Front, the two sides faced each other in rows of heavily fortified trenches. Both excavated tunnels and mines deep under enemy lines and packed them with explosives, ready to be detonated when an attack began. Counter-mines were dug to destroy enemy mines before they could be finished. Vast mines were exploded by the British at the Battle of the Somme on July 1, 1916, but their most effective use was at the start of the Battle of Messines on June 7, 1917.

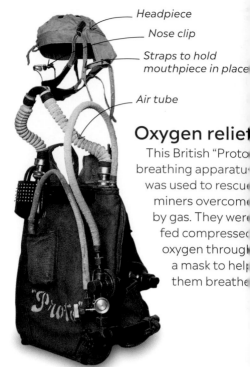

Headpiece
Nose clip
Straps to hold mouthpiece in place
Air tube

Oxygen relief
This British "Proto" breathing apparatus was used to rescue miners overcome by gas. They were fed compressed oxygen through a mask to help them breathe.

Sappers at work
British artist David Bomberg painted members of the Royal Engineers, known as sappers, digging and reinforcing this underground trench. Sappers ensured that trenches and tunnels were properly constructed and did not collapse.

Sappers used pulleys and levers to erect support timbers.

"It is horrible. You often wish you were dead, there is no shelter, we are lying in water... our clothes do not dry."
—German soldier, Passchendaele, 1917

Passschendaele

In 1917, British and Commonwealth troops planned to break through the German front line (known as the Ypres Salient) around Ypres, Belgium, and then go on to seize the Channel Ports used by German submarines. The first action was the Battle of Messines that began on June 7, 1917. After a huge artillery bombardment, 19 mines packed with one million tons of explosives blew up under the German lines on Messines Ridge. On July 31, British, French, Anzac, and Canadian troops attacked the Salient again. The Third Battle of Ypres, known as Passchendaele, was one of the bloodiest of the war. Heavy rain and mud hampered the attack, but it finally culminated in the capture of the village and ridge of Passchendaele on November 10, 1917.

Waterlogged

The clay soils around Ypres meant that water did not easily drain away, so defenses for trenches were often built above the ground by banking up earth and sandbags. Even so, in winter, the trenches were constantly flooded. Pumping out mines and trenches, as these Australian tunnelers are doing at Hooge in September 1917, was an essential task.

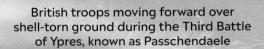

British troops moving forward over shell-torn ground during the Third Battle of Ypres, known as Passchendaele

Muddy quagmire

Heavy rainfall and constant shelling at Passchendaele created a deadly mud bath. Many injured men died as they were unable to lift themselves clear of the sticky mud. Stretcher bearers were barely able to carry the wounded to dressing stations.

Hawthorn Ridge

This British mine exploded under German lines at the Battle of the Somme, July 1, 1916. The Hawthorn Ridge explosion was captured on film (left) by photographer Geoffrey Malins. The mine was blown 10 minutes before Zero Hour, which warned the Germans of the impending attack.

The final year

In early 1918, the war looked to be turning in favor of Germany. Russia had withdrawn from the war, so Germany could now focus on the Western Front, and most US troops had yet to reach France. But the Allied blockade of its ports kept Germany short of vital supplies, food was scarce, and strikes and mutinies were rife. Ottoman Turkey, Bulgaria, and Austria-Hungary collapsed under Allied attack. By early November, Germany stood alone. On November 7, a German delegation crossed the front line to discuss peace terms with the Allies.

Brigadier General John Campbell addressing men of the 46th Division from Riqueval Bridge over the St. Quentin Canal in France

Russia pulls out

The Russian government became increasingly unpopular as the war progressed. In February 1917, a revolution overthrew the Tsar, but the new government continued the war. A second revolution in October brought the Bolshevik Party to power. A cease-fire was agreed with Germany, and in March 1918 Russia signed the Treaty of Brest-Litovsk and withdrew from the war.

Germans and Russians celebrate the cease-fire on the Eastern Front, 1917

French and British troops in action during the Ludendorff Offensive

The Ludendorff Offensive

General Ludendorff launched a huge attack on the Western Front on March 21, 1918, hoping to defeat Britain and France before US troops arrived. Germany advanced almost 40 miles (64 km) by July but suffered 500,000 casualties.

March 3 Treaty of Brest-Litovsk; Russia leaves the war
March 21 Vast Ludendorff Offensive on the Western Front

July 15 Last German offensive launched on the Western Front
July 18 French counterattack begins on the Marne

August 8 British launch offensive near Amiens
September 12 Americans launch offensive at St. Mihiel, France

September 14 Allies attack Bulgaria from Greece
September 25 Bulgaria seeks peace

Second Battle of the Marne

On July 18, 1918, French and US forces counterattacked against the German advance on the Marne River, east of Paris, and began to push the Germans eastward. By August 6, the Germans had lost 168,000 men, many buried where they fell on the battlefields (above). The Allies now had the upper hand.

French children march alongside the Allied army.

Soldiers of the 8th (Irish) Battalion, King's (Liverpool Regiment) marching through Lille, France, November 1918

Crossing the line

On August 8, 1918, a huge British, French, and Commonwealth offensive began near Amiens, France. Allied troops were pushing toward the heavily fortified Hindenburg Line, the Germans' fall-back defensive position. On September 29, the British 46th North Midland Division took the bridge at Riqueval. They had broken the Line at last and posed for this photograph.

The last days

By October 5, the Allies had breached the entire Hindenburg Line. Both sides suffered great casualties as the German Army was pushed steadily eastward. As the British and French recaptured towns and cities lost in 1914, including Lille (above), the German retreat was turning into a defeat.

September 27 British begin to breach Hindenburg Line
October 1 British take Ottoman Turkish-held Damascus

October 6 German government starts to negotiate an armistice
October 24 Italy attacks Austria-Hungary at Vittorio Veneto

October 29 German fleet mutinies
October 30 Ottoman Turkey agrees to an armistice
November 4 Austria-Hungary agrees to an armistice

November 9 The Kaiser abdicates
November 11 Armistice between Germany and the Allies; war ends

Armistice and peace

At 11 a.m. on the 11th day of the 11th month of 1918, the guns of Europe fell silent after more than four years of war. The Allies wanted to make sure that Germany would never go to war again. The eventual peace treaty redrew the map of Europe and forced Germany to pay huge damages to the Allies. German armed forces were reduced and Germany lost a great deal of land and all of its overseas colonies.

Carriage talks
On November 7, 1918, a German delegation met Marshal Foch, the Allied commander in chief in his railroad carriage in the forest of Compiègne, France. On November 11, they signed an armistice agreement.

Spreading the news
News of the Armistice spread around the world in minutes, in newspapers and telegrams, and by word of mouth in every neighborhood.

Vive la paix!
In Paris, US soldiers danced in an impromptu line as French citizens watched. In London, women and children danced in the streets while their men prepared to leave the front. In Germany, there was shock and relief that the fighting was over.

Signing the treaty

These soldiers watching the signing of the Treaty of Versailles had waited a long time for this moment. The Allies first met their German counterparts in January 1919. Negotiations almost broke down several times before a final agreement was reached in June 1919.

The Treaty of Versailles

The peace treaty that ended the war was signed in the Hall of Mirrors in the Palace of Versailles near Paris, on June 28, 1919. Irish artist William Orpen's painting shows heads of states, including the four Allied leaders—France's Georges Clemenceau, Britain's David Lloyd George, Italy's Vittorio Orlando, and the US's Woodrow Wilson—watching the German delegates sign the treaty.

The Treaty of Versailles

The peace treaties

The Treaty of Versailles was signed by representatives of the Allied powers and Germany. Over the year that followed, in the Allies' treaties with Austria, Bulgaria, Turkey, and Hungary, a new map of Europe emerged.

The cost of war

The human cost of this war was huge. Over 65 million men fought, of whom more than half were killed or injured—eight million killed, two million died of illness and disease, 21.2 million wounded, and 7.8 million taken prisoner or missing. About 6.6 million civilians also perished. Among the combatant nations, apart from the US, there was barely a family that had not lost at least one close relative. European economies were ruined, while the US emerged as a major world power.

Private Jack Mudd was a soldier in the London Regiment (Royal Fusiliers).

Flanders poppy

Elizabeth "Lizzie" Mudd

Mementos

Soldiers on both sides of the Western Front pressed wild flowers as mementos. Private Jack Mudd sent this red Flanders poppy to his wife, Elizabeth, before he was killed at Passchendaele. The poppies are featured in the wartime poem *In Flanders Fields* by Canadian Lieutenant Colonel John McCrae and inspired the British Legion to sell paper poppies to raise money for injured soldiers and as a sign of remembrance for the dead.

War memorials

The Western Front is lined with graveyards and memorials to the fallen. The Douaumont Ossuary in France contains the remains of around 130,000 unknown French and German soldiers who died during the Battle of Verdun.

Prussian Iron Cross

Victoria Cross (V.C.)

French *Croix de Guerre*

For gallantry

Every combatant nation awarded medals for bravery to its soldiers, civilians, and allies—including five million Iron Crosses in Germany, over two million *Croix de Guerre* in France, and more than 600 Victoria Crosses across the British Empire. Before 1918, Victoria Crosses given to Royal Navy recipients had blue ribbons, which were later changed to red ones.

Unknown warrior

Many of the dead were too badly disfigured to be identified. Thousands more just disappeared, presumed dead. The first two tombs of an unknown warrior were installed on November 11, 1920, and stand at the Arc de Triomphe, Paris, and Westminster Abbey, London (right).

The grave was filled in with 100 sandbags of earth from the battlefields.

Many soldiers painted to pass the time.

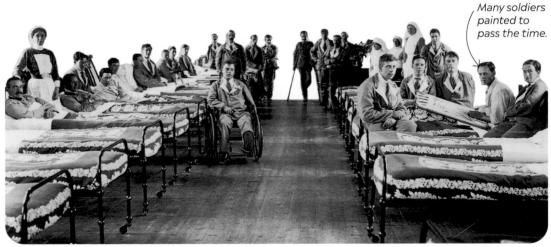

Care and recovery

For thousands of soldiers with life-changing injuries, reconstructive surgery helped treat facial injuries, masks and prosthetics replaced impaired or missing body parts, and artificial limbs gave some mobility. Some soldiers stayed in nursing homes for the rest of their lives.

Did you **know?**

BITE-SIZE FACTS

In 1917, British newspapers claimed that the explosion of mines at Messines Ridge at Ypres, Belgium, could be heard in London, 140 miles (220 km) away.

Every British soldier was given his boots in time to wear them in and, from the Somme onward, his own steel helmet. Specialist equipment was kept in communal stores—handed on from unit to unit.

Left to right, British Army specialist clothing for transport drivers, flame thrower operators, trench raiding (in winter camouflage), and airmen

Flame throwers were first used by the Germans. They fired jets of flame as far as 131 ft (40 m).

Russia had the largest army. It mobilized 12 million troops during the course of the war. More than three-quarters were killed, wounded, or went missing in action.

Built in 1915, the first prototype tank, "Little Willie," carried a crew of three and had a top speed of 3 mph (4.8 km/h). At first, British tanks were split into "males" and "females." Male tanks had cannons, while female tanks had heavy machine guns.

Tunnelers laid mines on the Western Front. Sometimes underground fights broke out, if they dug into an enemy tunnel by mistake.

Prague-born Walter Trier (1890–1951) produced political cartoons. The famous work above shows Europe in 1914 on the eve of World War I, with the national leaders threatening one another.

Filling a Thermos container that kept food hot

Map of Europe in 1914, drawn by cartoonist Walter Trier

Food was prepared in field kitchens that could be several miles behind the front line. It was impossible to take transport vehicles into the trench, so food had to be carried to the front on foot.

The Pool of Peace is a 40 ft (12 m) deep lake at Spanbroekmolen, near Messines, Belgium. It fills a crater made in 1917 when the British detonated a mine containing 45 tons of explosives (see p.57).

To help military communications, messenger dogs carried orders to the front line in capsules strapped to their bodies, while other dogs were trained to lay down telegraph wire!

A German messenger dog laying telegraph wire

Belgian soldiers firing artillery guns from behind camouflage screens during the war

QUESTIONS AND ANSWERS

Who was "Big Bertha"?

Weighing 96,342 lb (43,700 kg), "Big Bertha" was a howitzer used by the Germans in World War I. Its designer, Gustav Krupp, named the weapon after his wife. It took its crew of 200 men six hours or more to assemble. It could be transported to its firing position by tractor and could fire a 2,050 lb (930 kg) shell a distance of 9.3 miles (15 km). Big Bertha's first successes were at Liege in Belgium. The 12 forts ringing the city were destroyed in three days.

Why did soldiers keep animals?

Most animals that traveled with the army had a job to do. Mules, horses, oxen, and camels transported heavy supplies. Messenger dogs and pigeons carried important communications. Away from the front line, some soldiers kept animals for food—rabbits for the cooking pot or hens for their eggs.

Soldiers with their rabbits and chickens

How did soldiers camouflage themselves?

For the first time in a major conflict, soldiers made use of camouflage. They wore khaki uniforms that blended in with the background. Steel helmets were often painted with matte paint mixed with sand or sawdust so that they would not reflect the light; other times they were smeared with mud or covered with sacking from sandbags. Soldiers also used sacking or netting to hide their equipment from the reconnaissance aircraft patrolling the skies.

How did soldiers know when to put on their gas masks?

There were soldiers on lookout duty night and day. These sentries used whatever they could find to raise the alarm—bells, rattles, whistles, or their own voice. When the soldiers heard the alarm, they put on their gas masks as quickly as they could—hopefully before the deadly gas drifted into the trench.

A sentry on duty

Why were tanks called tanks?

While it was being developed, the tank was known as a "landship." However, there were fears that this name was too obvious, spies might wonder why so many of these objects were being produced, and the Germans might catch on to the new invention. The British had to come up with a believable name. They decided that, with its body shape, perhaps it could be passed off as a water storage tank, and called it a "tank" instead.

Sentry wears mask to protect from gas attack

Metal bell sounds the alarm

People and places

So many people played an important role in planning or fighting World War I, but here are some of the key names and battle sites.

President Raymond Poincaré of France · General Ferdinand Foch · General Joseph Joffre · King George V of Britain · General Sir Douglas Haig

IMPORTANT PERSONALITIES

Alexei Brusilov (1853–1926)
General Brusilov broke Austro-Hungarian lines in 1916 and took command of Russian forces on the Eastern Front in 1917.

Luigi Cadorna (1850–1928)
The general in charge of the Italian Army had only one success—the recapture of Gorizia in 1916.

Russian General Brusilov

Ferdinand Foch (1851–1929)
Artillery specialist Ferdinand Foch successfully led the French at the Marne. By 1918, he was coordinating all the Allied forces on the Western Front.

Anthony Fokker (1890–1939)
Dutch designer Anthony Fokker developed the first fighter plane with a forward-facing synchronized machine gun. Germany used 40 different Fokker aircraft during the war.

René Fonck (1894–1953)
Frenchman René Fonck was the Allies' most successful fighter pilot. He shot down 75 planes.

Douglas Haig (1861–1928)
Britain's top general on the Western Front was Sir Douglas Haig. He ordered the offensives at the Somme and Passchendaele, as well as the final, successful Allied offensive.

Paul von Hindenburg (1847–1934)
Early in the war, Paul von Hindenburg successfully led the war against the Russians. By 1916, he commanded all German land forces. His Hindenburg Line withstood attack from 1917 to 1918.

Joseph Joffre (1852–1931)
Joseph Joffre was Commander of the French Army. After heavy losses on the Western Front, he was replaced in 1916.

T. E. Lawrence (1888–1935)
"Lawrence of Arabia" led an Arab revolt against the Turks in the Middle East. Although Ottoman rule ended, his vision for independent Arab states was unsuccessful.

Rittmeister von Richthofen (1892–1918)
Germany's "Red Baron" shot down 80 planes—more than any other World War I pilot. He was shot down near Amiens.

Maximilian von Spee (1861–1914)
This German admiral sank two British cruisers off Chile. His own ship, the *Scharnhorst*, sank near the Falklands.

Gabriel Voisin (1880–1973)
French-born aircraft designer Gabriel Voisin is famous for his Voisin III (the first Allied plane to shoot down an enemy) and his Voisin V bomber, armed with a 37 mm cannon.

Margaretha Zelle (1876–1917)
Dutch-born "Mata Hari" denied being a double agent but may have spied for both the French and Germans. The French shot her in 1917.

Anthony Fokker with his Fokker DI aircraft

Propeller rotation was synchronized with gunfire

Aircraft designer Gabriel Voisin (right)

MAJOR BATTLES

Tanks during the Amiens offensive

Amiens
In August 1918, General Rawlinson led a successful Allied offensive to retake the Amiens Line in France. On the first day, the Allies advanced 7.5 miles (12 km).

Cambrai
General Haig took the Germans by surprise in November 1917 when he attacked them at Cambrai, France. At first, the Allies gained ground, but the Germans soon regained their position. The estimated casualties were 45,000 British soldiers and 50,000 Germans.

Gaza
In March 1917, General Dobell led a British attack on Turkish-held Gaza, a key port on the way to Palestine. Gaza finally fell in November, after bombardment from ships offshore.

A British dressing station at Cambrai

Heligoland Bight
In August 1914, British ships attacked German vessels near the naval base on Heligoland in the North Sea. In the ensuing battle, the British sank three cruisers and a destroyer.

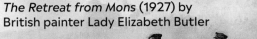
The Retreat from Mons (1927) by British painter Lady Elizabeth Butler

Jutland
May 1916 saw the war's only major sea battle, off the Danish coast of Jutland. Both sides claimed victory. The British suffered the heaviest losses, but had maintained control of the North Sea.

Mons
The British Expeditionary Force met the advancing German Army at Mons, France, in August 1914. The Germans suffered heavy losses but forced the British back to the Marne River.

Passchendaele
The Third Battle of Ypres, Belgium, (known as Passchendaele) began in July 1917. First, the Allies spent 10 days bombarding the Germans. Their advance slowed by torrential rain, they finally took the ridge in November.

Somme
The Battle of the Somme, France, lasted from July to November 1916. The Allies suffered 620,000 casualties (including 58,000 on the first day) and the Germans an estimated 500,000 casualties.

Verdun
The Germans attacked the garrison town of Verdun, France, in February 1916. They outnumbered the French five to one at first, but the battle ran on for 10 months and nearly a million died.

Vittorio Veneto
In one of the last offensives of the war, the Italians retook Vittorio Veneto on October 29, 1918. The battle, fought in Italy, ushered in the end of the war with Austria-Hungary.

Ypres
The Belgian town of Ypres was taken by the Germans in August 1914, but the British recaptured it in October. A second battle of Ypres took place in April and May 1915 and a third, Passchendaele, in 1917.

A British field kitchen at the Somme, 1916

Find out more

There are many ways you can find out more about World War I. Ask older generations of your family if they remember stories about relatives who fought in the war. You can find lots more information online and at your library. War museums, television documentaries, and old war movies also bring this part of history back to life.

Remembrance Day

Each year, on the Sunday nearest to November 11, services are held at local and national war memorials across the UK to commemorate the fallen.

French tricolor (national flag) is flown each year on November 11

The Tank Museum

The world's largest tank museum at Bovington, Dorset, is home to the first tank prototype, Little Willie, and runs lots of special events.

Arc de Triomphe

Built by Napoleon, the Arc de Triomphe in Paris, France, now keeps alive the memory of the millions of soldiers killed in World War I, marked by a flame of remembrance and the Tombe du Soldat inconnu (unknown soldier).

USEFUL WEBSITES

- An online international encyclopedia on World War I, with many articles written by leading experts: **encyclopedia.1914-1918-online.net**
- Easy-to-navigate site featuring videos, speeches, photographs, biographies, and more: **www.history.com/topics/world-war-i**
- A companion website to the PBS series on World War I, including multimedia effects: **www.pbs.org/wgbh/americanexperience/films/great-war/**

PLACES TO VISIT

SMITHSONIAN INSTITUTION, WASHINGTON, DC
• Explore the myths and realities of World War I combat. On exhibit are actual aircraft that took to the skies during World War I.

LIBERTY MEMORIAL MUSEUM KANSAS CITY, MISSOURI
• The only public museum in the US dedicated solely to the history of World War I. The collection includes gas masks, letters and postcards from the field, memorial paintings, and other artifacts.

IMPERIAL WAR MUSEUM, LONDON, UK
• World War I galleries showing how the war was fought and won, its impact on people's lives, and its far-reaching consequences.
• Over 1,300 objects on display, including weapons, uniforms, diaries, film, and art.
• The Lord Ashcroft Gallery: Extraordinary Heroes housing the world's largest collection of Victoria Crosses.

IN FLANDERS FIELDS MUSEUM, IEPER (YPRES), BELGIUM
• Museum dedicated to the war in Belgium, and the Ypres Salient.
• Thousands of original artifacts, including uniforms, weapons, and personal items.
• Visitors can follow the stories of individuals who fought there using a digital bracelet.

A still from the movie *1917*

War movies

Many movies have been made about World War I. Not all are based on solid fact, but usually they give a flavor of the time. One of the most critically acclaimed is *1917*, released in 2019. Directed by Sam Mendes, the movie was designed to be an immersive experience of the war.

Sculpture shows parents mourning the loss of their son

War monument

Many artists and writers have shared their feelings about World War I in their work. German artist Käthe Kollwitz (1867–1945) made this statue for the German war cemetery at Vladslo, Belgium. Her son, Peter, is buried there.

Anzac Day

In Australia and New Zealand, April 25, is Anzac Day. Parades and ceremonies mark the lives of the thousands of Anzac soldiers who died at Gallipoli, Turkey, in 1915.

Imperial War Museum, London

The Imperial War Museum's First World War Gallery tells the story of the war through its many artifacts and innovative media, from 1914 to its aftermath.

Trench signposts from World War I displayed at the Imperial War Museum

Glossary

Nurses wheel convalescent soldiers around the hospital grounds

ABDICATE Give up office or power.

ALLIANCE A group of nations or people with shared aims or interests, who have agreed to cooperate.

ALTITUDE Height above sea level.

AMMUNITION Bullets and shells fired from weapons.

AMPUTATION Surgical removal of a body part, such as an arm or leg.

ANZAC Member of the Australian and New Zealand Army Corps.

ARMISTICE End of hostilities. Armistice Day, now known as Remembrance Sunday, is commemorated each year on the Sunday closest to November 11.

ARMS RACE Rivalry between nations to build up weaponry, or armaments.

ARTILLERY Heavy weapons, such as field guns, and the sections of the armed forces that use them.

ASSASSINATION The murder of someone for political purposes.

BATTERY A number of artillery guns positioned to fire on the enemy.

BAYONET A blade fixed to a rifle or other firearm, to stab the enemy when fighting at close quarters.

BULLY BEEF A name for corned beef.

BUNKER An underground bomb shelter.

CAMOUFLAGE Coloring designed to blend in with the background. In World War I, this was mostly used to hide gun positions, or ships, although some soldiers blackened their faces before night patrols and snipers wore camouflaged suits.

CAVALRY Soldiers who fight on horseback.

CLIP A device for carrying and rapidly loading rifle ammunition.

COLONY A dependency, or place, which is ruled by a foreign nation.

CONSCIENTIOUS OBJECTOR Someone who refuses to fight for moral reasons.

CONSCRIPT Someone who is forced by law to fight in the army.

Small box respirator gas mask

CONVALESCENT Someone who has been seriously injured or ill and is slowly recovering.

CONVOY Merchant ships traveling together, protected by a naval escort.

CRYPTOGRAPHY The study and creation of secret codes.

DETONATE To explode or cause to explode.

DOGFIGHT An aerial battle between two fighter aircraft.

DYSENTERY An infection of the intestines that causes diarrhea and bloody feces and was responsible for many casualties.

EMPLACEMENT A mound or platform from which guns are fired.

ENLIST Join the armed forces.

ENTENTE A friendly agreement or informal alliance between nations.

An intelligence officer inspects aerial photographs of enemy trenches

EVACUATION Moving people away from a place where they are in danger.

FIELD GUN A mobile artillery gun used against men and trenches.

FLOTILLA A fleet or group of small ships.

FRONT LINE The border between enemy territories, where the fighting is.

FUSELAGE The body of an airplane.

GAS In the context of war, a poisonous gas, such as chlorine, used as a weapon to choke, blind, or kill the enemy.

GRENADE A small bomb hurled by hand.

GUERRILLA A fighter in a unit dedicated to sabotage and hit-and-run attacks. From the Spanish for "small war."

TOGETHER WE WIN

UNITED STATES SHIPPING BOARD ——— EMERGENCY FLEET CORPORATION

An American propaganda poster

HOWITZER An artillery gun that fired high.

INCENDIARY Describes a bomb, bullet, or other device designed to cause fire.

INFANTRY Foot soldiers.

INTELLIGENCE Useful military or political information, or the spies who gather it.

KNOT A unit for measuring a ship's speed. One knot equals 1.15 mph (1.85 km/h).

MACHINE GUN An automatic gun that fires bullets in rapid succession.

MEDICAL ORDERLY A soldier with some medical training.

MESS TIN A tin used by soldiers to eat their food. US soldiers called them "meat cans."

MINE A large underground chamber packed with explosives, placed under enemy lines by tunnelers, or sappers.

MOBILIZATION Preparation of troops for active service.

MORALE Strength of purpose, confidence, or faith.

MORSE CODE A code that represents letters of the alphabet by a sequence of dots and dashes, or long and short signals of light or sound. Named after inventor Samuel Morse (1791–1872).

MUNITIONS Stores of weapons and other military equipment.

NEUTRALITY The refusal to take sides.

NO-MAN'S-LAND An area between two opposing forces that has not been captured by either side.

NONCOMBATANT Someone serving but not fighting with the army, such as a chaplain or an army doctor.

PERISCOPE A device fitted with mirrors to allow the user to see things not in their direct line of sight.

PROPAGANDA Information intended to convince people of a specific viewpoint—in posters and broadcasts, for example.

RECONNAISSANCE Taking a preliminary look at an area before sending in troops, usually in order to locate the enemy.

RECONNOITRE To survey an area in preparation for a military advance.

RECRUIT Someone enlisted into the army.

REGULAR FORCES The professional soldiers, rather than reservists or wartime volunteers.

RESERVE FORCES People who are not part of the regular army but have been trained and are ready to be the first extra troops mobilized in an emergency.

German stereoscopic periscope

RESPIRATOR A device worn over the face to prevent the wearer from breathing in poisonous gas.

RIFLE A long-barreled gun, fired from shoulder level.

SALIENT A bulge in the front line, such as at Ypres, where the army has taken over some enemy territory.

SEAPLANE An aircraft fitted with floats or skis to land on or take off from water.

SHELL An explosive projectile that is fired from an artillery piece, such as a field gun or howitzer.

SHELL SHOCK Mental strain or illness suffered by a soldier who has fought in a war.

SHRAPNEL A type of anti-personnel projectile that contained small shot or spherical bullets, usually of lead, with an explosive charge to scatter the shot.

TELEGRAPH A communications device that transmits messages by means of electrical signals along a wire.

TORPEDO A self-propelled underwater missile fired from a boat or submarine.

TRENCH A ditch dug by soldiers for protection against enemy fire.

TRUCE An agreement to stop fighting.

U-BOAT A German submarine.

ULTIMATUM A final demand, which, if it is not met, results in serious consequences and a total breakdown of communication.

WAR BOND A certificate issued by a government in return for the investment of a sum of money. The money raised helps pay for the war and is repaid later with interest.

WAR OF ATTRITION Continuous attacks to wear down the enemy.

WIRELESS A communications device that sends messages as radio signals.

ZERO HOUR The starting time of an attack or military operation.

British 0.303 in Maxim Mark III medium machine gun, c. 1902

British 4.5-inch high-explosive shell

Index

Acknowledgments

The publisher would like to thank the following people for their help with making the book: Elizabeth Bowers, Christopher Dowling, Mark Pindelski, & the photography archive team at the Imperial War Museum for their invaluable help; the author for assisting with revisions; Claire Bowers, David Ball, Neville Graham, Rose Horridge, Joanne Little, and Susan Nicholson for the wallchart; BCP, Marianne Petrou, and Owen Peyton Jones for checking the digitized files; Bipasha Roy and Kathakali Banerjee for editorial assistance; Heena Sharma for design assistance; Hazel Beynon for proofreading; and Elizabeth Wise for the index.

The publisher would like to thank the following for their kind permission to reproduce their images:
(a=above, b=below/bottom, c=center, f=far, l=left, r=right, t=top)

akg-images: 36br, 52clb, 61tr, 7crb, 37cl, 38cl, 38bl, 42bl, 43bc, 38cl, 38bl, 59tr, Ullstein Bild 64tr; **Alamy Stock Photo:** Arterra Picture Library / Collection Philippe Clement 65t, CBW 21tr, 57cl, Chronicle 19tr, 21br, 25bc, 32bc, Granger, NYC 58c, Allan Hartley 69cr, History and Art Collection 13ca, IanDagnall Computing 8tr, Landmark Media 69tr, De Luan 58-59ca, Malcolm Park editorial 69bc, Military Images 13clb, PA Images 63cr, Science History Images 47tc, Shawshots 26–27c, The Print Collector / Heritage Images 42br, The Protected Art Archive 48–49c, Windmill Books \ UIG 31br, vint1 39tl, Michel & Gabrielle Therin-Weise 42cra, World History Archive 47cla;
Bovington Tank Museum: 68ca; **Bridgeman Images:** 60-61b, Lebrecht Authors 37bc, National Army Museum 23br, © Royal Hospital Chelsea, London, UK 67tr;
Collection of the Smithsonian National Museum of African American History and Culture: 55br; **Corbis:** 2tr,

49c; **Dreamstime.com:** Upixa2 15tc; **Dorling Kindersley:** Andrew L. Chernack, Springfield, Pennsylvania: 3tr, 55bc; Andy Crawford By permission of IWM (Imperial War Museums) 2cl, 24-25bc, Imperial War Museum 13cl, 20bl, 20br, 51tc, 70bc, 71tr, 71bl, 71br; National Army Museum: 44ca; RAF Museum, Hendon: 34tl, 34cl; Spink and Son Ltd: 3tl, 4tr, 43bl; **Getty Images:** Bettmann 20-21ca, 22cra, 27tr, 48br, 49bl, 55t, 60tr, Maj. Tracy Everts / US Army Signal Corps / Bettmann 44-45b, Corbis Documentary / Free Agents Limited 68bl, Corbis Historical 6tr, 34br, Corbis Premium Historical / Hulton Deutsch 43t, Ann Ronan Pictures / Print Collector / Hulton Archive 7tr, Hulton Archive / Apic 19br, 51l, Hulton-Deutsch Collection / Corbis 66br, Keystone-France / Gamma-Keystone 41tr, Swim Ink 2, LLC / Corbis 71tl, Universal History Archive / UIG 61ca, Sergeant J.J. Marshall / Library of Congress / Corbis / VCG 31tr; **mauritius images:** TopFoto 46b; **Robert Harding Picture Library:** Tim Graham 62-63c; **Heeresgeschichtliches Museum, Wien:** 8bl; **Hulton Getty:** 14cl, 19bl, 33ca, 34cb, 36cra, 41cr, 47bc, 50clb, 60cla, 61tr, Topical Press Agency 50bc; **By permission of IWM (Imperial War Museums):** 2tl, 9bl (Q81763), IItr (Q70075), 12clb (32002), 14bc (Q42033), 42tl (Cat. No. 0544), 16c (Q57228), 17br (E(AUS)577),18l (CO2533), 18tc (Q2953), 18br (IWM90/62/4), Brooks, Ernest (Lieutenant) (Photographer) 65br, IWM Art.IWM ART 1460 / Sargent, John Singer (Artist) 45tl, IWM Art.IWM ART 1656 / Nash, John 28tr, IWM MUN 3237 27crb, IWM ORD 101 / Vickers, Sons & Maxim 10-11b, IWM Q 106250 / Miller, David 32-33c, IWM Q 13637, Brooks, Ernest (Lieutenant) (Photographer) 41b, IWM Q 1462 / Brooks, Ernest (Lieutenant) (Photographer) 23t, IWM Q 193 / Royal Engineers No 1 Printing Company 16b, IWM Q 24087 28cb, IWM Q 2953 / Brooks, Ernest (Lieutenant) (Photographer) 19tc, IWM Q 4834 / Brooke, John

Warwick (Lieutenant) 64bc, IWM Q 70232 / Press Agency photographer 10-11t, IWM Q 823 / Brooks, Ernest (Lieutenant) (Photographer) 15bl, IWM Q 8477 / McLellan, David (Second Lieutenant) (Photographer) 23cb , The Menin Road by Paul Nash 19cb(Cat. No. 2242), 19cla, 19bc, 22bl (CO1414), 24c, 26bl (Q104), 27cr (E921), 28cl, 29tl (Q1561), 29crb (Q739), 28-29b (Q53), 30tr (Q1778), 30cl (Q2628), 321, 33tc (Q30678), 33cr (Q19134), 34crb (Q42284), 34bc (Q69593), 34-35c, 36clb, 37 (Q27488), 38tr (PST0515), 39ca (Q20883), 39br (Q63698), 41tl (Q13618), 40br (Q13281), 40cl (Q13603), 45cra (Q55085), 48bl, 50c (Q26945), 52bl (Q9364), 53cr (Q6434), 53br (Q9364), 54tl (2747), Sappers at Work by David Bomberg 56cl (2708), 57tr (E(AUS)1396), 57cr (Q5935), 56-57b (Q2708), 58clb (Q10810), 59crb (Q9586), The Signing of Peace in the Hall of Mirrors, Versailles by Sir William Orpen 61tl (2856), 64cla (Q30788), 64crb (Q50671), 65clb (Q10956), 66tr (Q949), 66cla (Q54534), 66bl (Q66377), 67tl (Q7302), 67clb (Q9631), 67br (Q1582), 70tl (Q27814), 70cr (Q26946); **Popperfoto:** Reuters 69clb; **Roger-Viollet:** 9tr, 9cr, llbr, 13cr, 19tl; Boyer 17bl; **Shutterstock.com:** Everett Collection 46c, Sam Shere / The LIFE Picture Collection 35bc; **Topham Picturepoint:** 46tl, 47r, 63b; **Ullstein Bild:** 8-9c.

All other images © Dorling Kindersley